PURSUE
OVERTAKE
RECOVER

PURSUE
OVERTAKE
RECOVER

**HOW TO RECLAIM
EVERY BLESSING
THAT HAS BEEN
LOST OR STOLEN
BY THE ENEMY**

KERRY KIRKWOOD

Unless otherwise identified, Scripture quotations are taken from the NEW AMERICAN STANDARD BIBLE®, Copyright © 1960, 1962, 1963, 1968, 1971, 1972, 1973, 1975, 1977, 1995 by The Lockman Foundation. Used by permission.

Scripture quotations marked KJV are from the King James Version.

Scripture quotations marked NKJV are from the New King James Version. Copyright © 1982 by Thomas Nelson, Inc. Used by permission. All rights reserved.

Scripture quotations marked NIV are from THE HOLY BIBLE, NEW INTERNATIONAL VERSION®, NIV® Copyright © 1973, 1978, 1984, 2011 by Biblica, Inc.™ Used by permission. All rights reserved worldwide.

Scripture quotations marked NLT are from the Holy Bible, New Living Translation, copyright © 1996, 2004, 2015 by Tyndale House Foundation. Used by permission of Tyndale House Publishers, Inc., Carol Stream, Illinois 60188. All rights reserved.

All emphasis within Scripture quotations is the author's own.

DESTINY IMAGE₀ PUBLISHERS, INC.
P.O. Box 310, Shippensburg, PA 17257-0310
"Promoting Inspired Lives."

This book and all other Destiny Image and Destiny Image Fiction books are available at Christian bookstores and distributors worldwide.

Cover design by: Eileen Rockwell
Interior design by Susan Ramundo

For more information on foreign distributors, call 717-532-3040.
Or reach us on the Internet: www.destinyimage.com.

ISBN 13 TP: 978-0-7684-1947-4
ISBN 13 EBook: 978-0-7684-1948-1
LP ISBN: 978-0-7684-1949-8
HC ISBN: 978-0-7684-1950-4

For Worldwide Distribution, Printed in the USA
1 2 3 4 5 6 / 21 20 19 18

DEDICATION

I dedicate this book to the millions who have waited long and prayed fervently for the redemption and recovery of lost family and lost health. To those who have lost hope while not seeing any change, as you read these pages may you find hope and courage to declare once again that you will pursue and recover all. I pray you will recognize a promise is not a wish list but a true Word from God that will take you to your appointment. Many of you will discover your disappointments have turned into appointments. Job 14:7-9 *"For there is hope for a tree, if it is cut down that it will sprout again, and that its tender shoots will not cease. Though its root may grow old in the earth, and its stump may die in the ground, yet at the scent of water it will bud and bring forth branches like a plant"* (NKJV).

There will be many of you who will sprout again after a loss or injustice. God keeps better books than we do. May the Lord grant you a fresh scent of water so you can taste and see your hope of a prosperous future is still in play. Since God is redemptive, and He never gives up on us, then why should we give up on His Promises? I dedicate this book to those who feel you have been cut back to the root. Get ready because there is rain in your forecast.

This book is a reflection of my wife, Diane. She never ceases to remind me of the seed sown in prayer towards the things we are waiting to see recovered. She is a constant in a world of unbelief and uncertainty. Her insistence on breaking through has led us into many new paths that would not have been discovered without her persistence. Diane; I love walking out this exciting journey of pursuing, overtaking, and now we are seeing many things being recovered.

ACKNOWLEDGMENTS

Anyone who has undertaken a project such as this understands the team effort and necessity of support. The Trinity Fellowship staff has been invaluable in the writing of this manuscript. They have taken on extra responsibilities and done so with joy. Their dedication and consistent service have afforded me the time and focus to do what I am called to do and what we as a corporate Body of Christ are called to do. Their service has always been so with an extreme sense of joy. Tina Smith, our office manager, goes beyond a normal job description to accomplish any and all tasks thrown her way. Duane Hett is the best executive pastor any senior pastor could ever hope for. He has been on the cutting edge of keeping us updated with the latest in technology. His invaluable expertise has kept us all sane by keeping all devices functioning. Pastor Jim Hahn is a gift from God to me. He is not only an associate pastor but goes beyond description. Besides preaching powerfully with sensitive and timely messages, he has a pastor's heart through and through. Pastor Franky Benitez has taken us many times to unforgettable heights as a worship pastor but has stepped up to take on many roles to further expedite my time to finish this project. There are many department leaders who have shown their faith and love for Trinity Fellowship that are too numerous to mention but just know you are woven into this book.

I also am very thankful for all the Antioch Oasis Network of pastors and leaders who have forged a strong bond with one another. Many of us have served in this network of churches and ministries for over twenty years. Pastor Olen Griffing, who founded the network and gathered leaders from around the world, has been a spiritual father to me in all seasons of ministry. Pastor Olen has challenged me to go beyond what I thought I could do, to see what God could do through me. For all the AOI Pastors who have allowed me the privilege to share the message you will find in this book, you are a part of forging this book in me.

Finally, to all those who I have come across in traveling to various venues of ministry, you are part of this writing. You have encouraged me through your purchase of messages related to the Power of Redemption. It is because of your hunger for the Word of God that pressed me forward to take the series on Redemption and Restoration to the next level of publication. I am very grateful for all the compliments that some thought went unnoticed or unheard. Your words have made a difference in seeing this to completion.

CONTENTS

INTRODUCTION

YEARS AGO, MY WIFE, Diane, and I were in Houston, Texas, having dinner with a pastor. The waiter walked up to the table and asked, "Is that red Envoy your car?"

"Yes," I said.

"Did you drive here with a busted window?"

"No."

"Well, you have one now," he said.

We rushed out to see that the window was indeed broken and my briefcase and Diane's tote bag had been stolen. We returned to the hotel feeling sick inside and a sense of being violated. The helpless feeling of being a victim was trying to find a foothold in my mind. My Bible and everything I needed for the next day to minister was gone. Though the perpetrators were looking for a computer, nonetheless it became personal to us.

Along with my Bible were research notes and the beginning of a manuscript. Houston, Texas, is a vast city and finding our possessions was like the proverbial needle in a haystack. When we returned to our hotel room, we were licking our wounds and trying to decide our next move. The discouragement of the loss was beginning to creep in and paralyze our thinking.

As we paced around the hotel room praying for wisdom while thinking maybe we should go and buy new Bibles for the next day of ministry, suddenly, the Lord gave Diane a word. He said, "Pursue and overtake and recover all. Do not allow thievery to be the norm. Do not allow what has been stolen from you to be lost." I recognized the passage coming from First Samuel 30 while David was in Ziklag and the Amalekites had stolen everything from David and his men.

So we prayed and called out for the spirit of redemption, "Lord, You've redeemed us from the curse of the law, and this has certainly been a curse, so we call those things that are not as though they are—we call them back in." The more we prayed for the recovery of everything and to not settle for the loss, the stronger in faith we felt.

This was back in the day before cell phones but we had an answering machine at home so I called to check the messages, just in case someone found the briefcase and the tote bag, where Diane kept her reading materials.

To our pleasant surprise, a man who owned a barbershop about a mile from the hotel had called. He said when he went out to empty the trash he saw a briefcase and a book, it was one that Diane was reading, and he thought, *Who would throw that away?* So he looked closer and found all the contents of the briefcase and tote! Since there was no computer in my briefcase, the thieves dumped everything in a large, commercial dumpster.

He left his phone number and address. When I went to recover the lost items, he told me, "I'm a lay preacher, and I took the liberty of copying some of your notes—if you don't mind."

The Lord spoke to us about being willing to reclaim things the enemy has stolen or is holding in darkness. According to James 1:17, *"Every good and every perfect gift is from above, coming down from the Father of the heavenly lights, who does not change like shifting shadows"* (NIV).

God, the Father of lights, sends good and perfect gifts to us—His children of lights. But between the Father of lights and the children of lights, there is the prince of the power of the air that causes disruption and hindrances, and sometimes prevents gifts from reaching fulfillment. We read in Daniel 10 in the Bible that Daniel had to pull out of darkness what God released in light. What God had said from there doesn't always get to us, not because God didn't send it, but because it is disrupted, interrupted somewhere between there and here.

When you realize God wants redemption in every part of your life, there is nothing that can hold you back from reclaiming whatever has been lost. He wants to restore you to fullness. God has given you four weapons in your redemption battle:

- Life in the blood

- Life in the seed

- Life in the Word

- Life in the tongue

The only weapon that can be used *for* you or *against* you is the power of the tongue. All the other weapons are offensive, but if you don't understand how to use this weapon, it can quickly turn against you.

You have the right to reclaim what has been lost in your life: relationships, finances, employment, health, etc. Believers are redeemed and you were bought, purchased through the blood of Christ. Redemption is not just about going to Heaven. Redemption is not just what He bought (the price of His own blood) you back from, but what He's taking you to. And the power of redemption is life-changing.

We will examine four particular areas of redemption the Bible talks about—so you can pursue, overtake, and recover all! In this book, you will discover the tools you need to not only proclaim what was lost but how to reclaim the things you have redemptive rights for. As you read through these pages, take note of what the Holy Spirit brings to mind that perhaps you have given up on or have simply written off as a loss. First Corinthians 4:5 says, *"Judge nothing before the time, until the Lord comes; whom will both bring to light the hidden things of darkness and reveal the counsels of the hearts. Then each one's praise will come from God."* (NKJV). The enemy will attempt to blind or hide what the Lord has given to you. God doesn't write it off because it is still there only hidden until we pursue what is ours and demand the thief to give them back.

CHAPTER I

YOUR REDEEMED RIGHTS

THE FIRST TIME I remember hearing the word "redemption" was as a young guy about ten years of age. When we went to the grocery store, the clerk would give my mom little green stamps, the number of stamps she received was based on the total grocery bill.

At home, my mother would put the stamps in a drawer and then when the drawer was full, my job was to use a wet sponge and paste them into special redemption books. When we had enough to "redeem," I would look in the S&H Green Stamp catalog, which was full of all sorts of things. When I found something I wanted, like a bicycle, I would circle my prize and crease the page that it was on. However, my mother quickly let me know she was saving for something for her kitchen.

When she had enough completed books, we would go to the S&H Redemption Center. I would carry the sack of stamp books. I felt like I was worth a million bucks. The clerk would look through each book to make sure every page was full of stamps. And then the book would be marked and stamped "Redeemed." It was fun! We didn't have much money back then, and I remember the time we got a blender and how many books it took to get it. I wanted to stick everything in that blender—I was a "juicer" long before it was popular.

REDEMPTION 101

The power of redemption can have a profound, life-changing effect. The word "redemption" today doesn't mean as much as during biblical times. Back then, redemption was a legal term, and it's important to understand that because the devil is a legalist. He accuses you before God every chance he gets.

Redemption in biblical times was a way of life and part of the law. It meant to buy back or pay the ransom; but more than that, it meant the original owner never loses the right to redeem it. It had to be the original owner who would redeem it, not someone else down the line. The original owner had first rights to refuse the redemption or choose to pay the redemptive price required. Only after the original owner gave up their rights to reclaim the property, could another buy the property or possession.

In the very beginning, God placed Adam in a Garden called Eden (Gen. 2:8). Eden means the place of His presence and the Place of His pleasure. God had given Adam full authority to govern God's creation. Only Adam had the authority to give up his authority to rule to another. Lucifer lost his place in Heaven and was looking for a way to gain a placement to rule in earth. Because God had placed Adam in that position, lucifer could not have any power or authority until the governing authority (Adam) was unseated.

Ephesians 4:27 strongly tells us to *"not give place to the devil"* (NKJV). The word place is *Topos* in the original text meaning ground or geography.[1] In essence, we are instructed to not give the devil any ground or territory from which he can dominate us. Any foothold we give up becomes an inroad in which we lose health, family, or even financial leverage.

While Adam was living under the authority of God, he was able to see all that God had given. He looked through the filter of glory. He and his wife were physically covered with the light of God.

The devil first introduced the thought to Eve that perhaps there was something outside of God. The thought was introduced into their thinking; *"has God really said"* (Gen. 3:1). When the question took root in their minds, and they acted on that thought to become independent of God, something flipped.

Instead of being dominated by the Spirit of God, they now became dominated by their souls. Their mind, will, and intellect has now taken over. Rationality has become the new norm. The next thing to happen was their eyes were opened to another world. Instead of seeing through the lens of the Father of light, they saw through the eyes of the prince of darkness. The light of glory left them, and they no longer could see what God had given them.

Today, the enemy still attempts to block us from seeing what God has given to us as His promise. Second Corinthians 4:4 says, "Whose minds the god of this age has blinded, who do not believe, lest the light of the gospel of the glory of Christ, who is the image of God, should shine on them." (NKJV). We see this also in Matthew 16:18 when Jesus says to Peter, "The gates of hell will not prevail against [the church]" (ESV). Notice Jesus says gates (plural) of hell. He was not referring to the place where at the end of the age the devil and his angels will be cast into the lake of fire. That hell has one gate in and no gate out. Jesus is using a form of hell, which means "anything that blocks the light." This is a stunning thought to consider.

Anything that keeps you from seeing your rights as a believer and your ability to see what God has given you can be a gate of hell. For example, in Matthew 16:23, Jesus began to teach his close disciples concerning what was coming. He expounded how He was to suffer from the hands of the chief priests and scribes and ultimately be killed. Peter took Jesus aside and rebuked Him. Peter didn't have eyes to see this happening. Peter had another agenda for Jesus staying alive. Jesus recognizing that Peter was being a gate of hell trying to keep him from His destiny said; *"Get behind me satan! You are an offense to me, for you are not mindful of the things of God, but things of men"* (Matt. 16:23 NKJV). Peter had no idea of the depth of what he was saying.

There may be someone who has said something to you that would cause you to give up on reclaiming your life in the fullness of God's desire. I pray you can see it for what it is even well-meaning as it might be, if it is still blocking the light to see your possessions in God.

Adam had no idea what he was giving up by simply letting another voice enter his family.

He made a decision in The Garden to give away his rights of all that God had honored him with. When Adam and Eve disobeyed God, sin entered into humanity, and we went from paradise to slavery. Slavery meant that from then to now we are under a worldly government, not a spiritual, godly government; a flawed authority, not the righteous authority of God; the kingdom of darkness and slavery, not the Kingdom of light and life. What the first Adam gave up in the Garden of Eden, it would take Jesus the second Adam to overcome in the Garden of Gethsemane.

Because of God's mercy and love, redemption gives us the power and right to access the Kingdom of Heaven that nothing else does. If we don't understand the power of redemption, we really can't fully enjoy and delight in everything God has done for us.

Knowing the importance of redemption means you will pray differently and under the authority of the power of the Holy Spirit. Your prayers will be very focused as you pray by the leading of the Holy Spirit. Your prayers will be redemptive. Redemptive thinking is realizing that although the enemy may have stolen your peace, property, or power, everything God gave you originally will eventually come back to you when it's redeemed. Hallelujah!

REDEMPTIVE THINKING

Humans are linear thinkers; it's our nature. We think in terms of something beginning at one particular time; we follow a timeline, dates on a calendar, and keep track by minutes, hours, days, years, and then, "all good things come to an end." God doesn't think in flat-line linear terms; God is a redemptive thinker. He thinks more circular.

The Bible describes Him as the Alpha and Omega (see Rev. 1:8; 21:6; 22:13). That doesn't just mean He is the beginning and the end, it means He ends where He began—never beginning and never ending. Isaiah 46:10 gives us insight into this circular thinking; it says, *"Declaring the end from the beginning, and from ancient times things which have not been done, saying, 'My purpose will be established and I will accomplish all My good pleasure.'"* So when He says we're closer now than when we first believed, that is redemptive thinking. When we think of Alpha or beginning, Omega has already seen the end. The Alpha moves toward the Omega and they meet as to say the beginning is the end and the end is now the beginning.

Prophecy doesn't move in a linear straight line but instead it moves closer toward the completion by moving toward the beginning. Something is renewed meaning it becomes like it was originally made. Redemptive thinking is prophetic because it is seeing things to be as it was originally intended to be. One of the best redemptive thinking examples is found in Ecclesiastes 1:7, *"The wind swirls about continually and comes again on its circuit. All the rivers run into the sea, yet the sea is not full; to the place from which the rivers come, there they return again"* (NKJV).

Redemptive thinking gives insight into the truth that nothing is gone but it is not seen. I hope this doesn't sound like some new age theology because it's not, but instead, very real. I tend to pray things that I know are available. If I don't think something is in store for me, I probably won't pursue taking it back.

So if we understand redemptive thinking, we pray prophetically because we see where God wants us to end up, not just where we are at the moment. Linear thinking is, "Well, it's been twenty years since the problem began, so I guess nothing's going to change." Therefore, we remain in the same condition, situation, and circumstance. But redemptive thinking awakens our soul. When Adam and Eve sinned, our soul, our spiritual being, actually went to sleep.

There was a movie many years ago that I didn't see but I liked the title, *Dead Men Walking*. From what I've read, it's about prison inmates and guards trying to survive during a biotoxin outbreak. The men infected were sure to die—they were "dead men walking." People who live in sin are dead people walking. They're dead in their trespasses, their sins, as the Bible says, and so, it takes an awakening by the Spirit of God, which is the power of redemption, to bring them into an understanding that something has changed (see Rom. 6:1,11; Rev. 1:5).

On December 18, 1865, the Thirteenth Amendment to the United States Constitution was ratified and Congress repealed slavery. By all historical facts, on that day, slavery was illegal in the United States. It was illegal to buy or own slaves, but more than a year later, there were slaves who had never heard the news they were free. Though by law they were free, by nature they didn't know if they were free or not. Some slave owners refused to tell the slaves they had been freed, they could live the life of freedom God called them to live. They didn't know they now could enjoy the unalienable rights God had granted them.

Yet when some slaves were freed, they felt more comfortable staying where they were rather than walking into freedom. The familiarity of slavery for some was safer than the unknown life set before them. This lifestyle of freedom in uncharted territory was to set a new course for generations to come. Others who would follow were depending on them to step out—not step back. The power of redemption is not just for us but for all those who will follow our example of pursuing all God has promised. It's a time of redemption; though unfamiliar and misunderstood it is available to all who will go after it.

In the same way that slaves were held in physical bondage, millions of people today are being held in spiritual bondage. Too many people don't realize Jesus is the Great Redeemer. Instead of passing up His right of redemption; He paid the ransom price—the life of one for the lives of all who would receive His redemption. The power of His blood destroyed the devil's claim of ownership over us. What was lost with Adam was reclaimed through Christ our Redeemer.

You don't have to put up with devil-induced afflictions. Linear thinkers give up, and think, "*Well, this is the way life is, I just need to settle in and accept it.*" You don't have to just lie down, and take it anymore, but instead, list what you want to reclaim whether it's your health, lost wages, or lost relationships. When you know what you want to reclaim, you can start to proclaim that your Redeemer lives. You have been made free, you are now a citizen of the Kingdom of Heaven, and you have rights in the throne room of God. You are redeemed by the blood of Jesus; this means you also have the right to redeem what was taken. Not only are you redeemed, but everything that was intended for you originally can be reclaimed because you have legal standing in the Courts of Heaven.

When we understand the truth of redemption, we move in a whole new level of praying, anointing, living, and giving. Only the next of kin could redeem or buy back and restore it to its original order. Acts 3:19 says, *"Therefore repent and return, so that your sins may be wiped away, in order that times of refreshing may come from the presence of the Lord."* Verse 21 continues, *"Whom the heaven must receive until the times of restoration of all things, which God has spoken by the mouth of all His holy prophets since the world began."* Revelation 21:5 says, *"He who sat on the throne said, 'Behold I will make all things new'"* (NKJV). Notice He didn't say I will make new things, but instead He is taking the things that were made originally and refurbishing them to the manufacturer's original specifications. What was corrupted by the Fall of Man is made new through the redemption of Christ. I hope you are beginning to see your redemption is not just about you going to Heaven someday. That is part of it but we don't have to wait for someday because your redemption is now.

I remember years ago giving a word over a family about a financial inheritance taken from them generations ago. I didn't understand what the inheritance was. All I knew was God wanted them to pursue something that belonged to them. It could have been anything or it could have been something spiritual that was not received. The Holy Spirit reminded them later of something that was in their family but wasn't researched. They discovered there had been money not yet distributed from a family trust. Had they not realized there was something out there belonging to them, they would have never gone searching for it.

If slaves didn't realize they had been set free, they would have stayed in captivity. Many don't realize God has appointed them to carry the Spirit of the Redeemer, so they can see what is theirs from the past, in the present and into the future.

But under redemption, you have the power to claim the inheritance of the family that has redeemed you and brought you into the royal lineage of the King.

REDEMPTION IS PROPHETIC

In Revelation 19:10, John saw this in Heaven, *"I fell at his feet to worship him, but he said to me, 'See that you do not do that! I am your fellow servant, and of your brethren who have the testimony of Jesus. Worship God! For the testimony of Jesus is the spirit of prophecy'"* (NKJV). Prophecy is a proceeding word or thoughts that moves ahead of us and acts as a catalyst. A catalyst is when something is added to existing substance that accelerates the process. When the Word of God is mixed with faith (Heb. 4:2) it becomes a proceeding word not a dormant word. Let me say it like this. When the Word and the Spirit unite inside you, there is a catalyst.

There may be promises you hold on to but have not seen any movement toward fulfillment, then, you need a catalyst. The Holy Spirit will bring to your remembrance (John 14:25) the things Jesus has said. The spirit of prophecy is a word awakened by the Spirit of Truth for you to use before the throne of grace to reclaim what belongs to you. The Holy Spirit will be much like an attorney in a courtroom advising you of your rights as a citizen. The accuser or prosecutor is the devil who attempts to keep you in a lower position than what you were redeemed for.

John 8:32 says, *"You shall know the truth and the truth shall make you free"* (NKJV). It's not the truth you hear that makes you free but the truth you apply. The spirit of prophecy will make you aware of what you have been given but also how to apply the power of redemption to see restitution restored to you.

Prophecy is what Jesus our Redeemer has already said. You are only saying what He has said about you. The Bible is full of prophetic promises you have a right as a redeemed one to claim. For instance, instead of rehashing how bad your children are, prophesy the promise from Isaiah 54:13, *"All your children shall be taught of the Lord, and great peace shall be of your children"* (ESV). Now you have a catalyst. The Word coupled with the Spirit will start the promise of redemption over your family. As long as I agree with the enemy as to the failure and fate of my children, then I am prophesying from the dark side of fear and not from the light side of redemption. Prophecy is seeing things from the point of redemption not from the lens of slavery.

I needed some wisdom to deal with a particular situation in my life. I spent time praying about it without any change. One evening while driving home from an out of town meeting, I felt the prompting of the Holy Spirit say to me that I should prophesy over myself. My first thought was that I knew myself too well to be accurate. Immediately the Holy Spirit said "you don't know yourself as much as you think." Then I was reminded of the verse which says that my spirit in me knows better than I know me (1 Cor. 2:11).

So by faith I started speaking as I have done over others many times before. I was totally shocked at the things I heard myself say about myself. Though it was a little strange at first, I soon witnessed that it was seed from another realm I needed to hear. I could now believe for things beyond what I could ask on my own or even allow my mind to venture into. I now have Word and Spirit to use as legal precedent to stand on. So when I prayed, I was no longer praying about it, but instead I was proclaiming what had already been redeemed for me. I only had to lay claim to it through faith.

Redemption is the currency of Heaven. Redemption gives us access not just into the heavenly, but into the very throne room of God. By the power of redemption, we see things in a whole different realm. The power of redemption allows us to see what God has in storage for us just waiting for us to lay claim to it. Prophetic people see what's ahead and what's coming so we can move toward what we see. *"Hope deferred makes the heart, sick"* (Prov. 13:12 NIV). Also, redemptive power allows you to give toward what your future is. You have a hope and a future. You can look beyond where you are right now and can sow toward what will be and what God has called you to move into. You can pursue your God-given destiny with a restored expectation.

YOU WERE MADE TO BE FEARED

If we understand the rights of those redeemed by the blood of Christ, we would pray with great confidence. We would never have any doubt or allow the devil to abuse us. The depth of this has taken some time to work past my theological mind to get deep into my spirit.

During a time of worship, while my heart was set upon the goodness of God and all that He has done for people I know; He surprised me with this statement. "Kerry, do you know I have created you to be feared?" This was not making sense to me because I would rather be liked and not feared. I want my children to love and respect me but I don't want them or anyone else to fear me.

I was obviously thinking in natural flesh and blood realms while God was speaking in realms of the Spirit. I was reminded of Psalm 139:14 which says *"I am fearfully and wonderfully made."* I have always only equated this verse to meaning something else. It actually means He has created us to be fearful. This doesn't mean we are to be full of fear but quite the opposite.

We were created with His specifications, and His DNA or Spirit was breathed into us to give us a part of Himself. When the devil sees you, he doesn't see flesh and blood the way we would recognize one another. He sees something that strikes fear inside of him. He sees the purchase price that severed his headship over us. He sees the blood that speaks to him and reminds him he is trespassing on holy ground. In the same way, when the Hebrews placed the blood of a lamb over the doorposts of their house (Exod. 12) and the angel of death had to pass over the house because of the blood covenant God had made. The devil sees the most powerful authority ever given to anyone; he sees the authority of the resurrection.

Isaiah 14 describes lucifer as a covering Cherub that was in the throne room of God. He saw the Glory of God and the power of that glory. Because he wanted this for himself, he was cast out of Heaven into the planet of darkness. Every time the devil and his minions see you, they see the glory deposited in you through redemption and they know how powerful that glory is and they can never access that place of glory again. Colossians 1:27 says, *"To them God willed to make known what are the riches of the glory of this mystery among the Gentiles; which is Christ in you, the hope of glory"* (NKJV). I hope you can see how huge this is. Let me boil it down to this; when the devil sees you, he is seeing what he lost in the throne room of God and will never again encounter. He knows how powerful the glory and the blood of the Lamb is.

The devil is fearful of you—especially when you catch the revelation of how fearful you are. Once this truth gets down deep inside you; you will pray differently and you will cast out demons with less frustration and a new renewed sense of the authority that comes through your redemptive rights.

The whole message of redemption hovers on this single issue of the blood. The blood of Jesus is not just a doctrinal belief; it is more real than anything you can imagine. It's the currency of Heaven. Ephesians 2:13 says, *"But now in Christ Jesus you who were once far off have been brought near by the blood of Christ"* (NKJV). We are no longer carrying on a long distance love relationship because we have been brought near through the redemptive price of the blood of the Lamb.

The only way the devil can defeat you is to blind you from how fearful he really is of you because of the One who lives inside you. You are more than a bag of bones, you are the sanctuary of the Most High God. The same creator that spoke creation into existence is now inside you. The devil is like a bully who tries to intimidate a child and then, suddenly, the bully turns and runs like a whimpering coward because he sees your big brother standing behind you. *"Greater is he that is in you than he that is in the world"* (1 John 4:4 KJV).

When you pray knowing you carry the blood and glory inside, you can access the throne of grace with boldness. The currency of Heaven truly has been bought, paid for, and now given to us to use as a prophetic voice on earth as it is in Heaven.

Everything changed that day when Jesus, the perfect sacrifice, was suspended between Heaven and earth. He was between the earth that was controlled by darkness and Glory set before Him. He was the intercessor who stood between bondage and freedom.

Matthew 27:48-53 records that day when hell had to set free their victims. Permit me to walk you through a sequence of events so you can see how much you are loved by God and feared by the devil. In verse 48, Jesus was offered sour wine to drink. On the surface, this wouldn't be significant, but once we need to understand that He was breaking generational curses. Ezekiel 18:2 says, no longer will you be able to say *"the fathers have eaten sour grapes and the children's teeth set on edge"* (NKJV). This idiom was used to explain the reason for generational curses; by saying "we are paying for the sins of our fathers." Jesus drinks the sour wine as to say no more will you pay for the sins of your father because I am bearing the sins of your fathers on the altar of the cross. You are now under redemption and no longer under servitude of our forefathers' sin.

Next in verse 50, Jesus cries out and yields up His Spirit and the veil of the Temple is torn; and the Presence of God was exposed to the rest of mankind. For the very first time, mankind could see the mercy seat where the blood was placed yearly for the nation. Not only was the veil torn from top to bottom, but an earthquake took place and the graves were opened of the saints who had died before the resurrection.

Take note of all that happened when the ransomed price had been paid. The powers of darkness had to let loose its captives. The devil lost his rights and those who were redeemed received their rights as citizens of the Kingdom of God. The kingdom of darkness lost and the Kingdom of Heaven took back ownership. The apostle Paul says it like this in Ephesians 4:8 *"When He ascended on high, He led captivity captive and gave gifts to men"* (NKJV). Before Jesus ascended, He first descended into the lower parts of the earth (v. 9). Jesus took back what had been captive and has made an edict in Heaven; He says all the captives who have accepted and received the blood of Jesus Christ is under a completely different government now. And those who are under the government of God have authority over the enemy's government that kept them in bondage.

When I enter another country, I show my passport, and I am soon made aware I am a guest in that nation and subject to all the laws and regulations of that government. I have no rights as a visitor there. However, in the Kingdom of God, the power of redemption says you are a citizen and have all the rights the power of redemption has given you—not because you deserve it, but because He delights in you having it.

PURSUE, OVERTAKE, AND RECOVER ALL

First Samuel 30:2-8 is a unique story of understanding how redemptive leaders see and think. David and his men had returned to their home base at Ziklag only to find all his family and possessions had been taken captive or burned, and all the men who served with him in battle had lost their families and possessions as well.

Can you imagine the sense of anger and depression that set on these mighty men? Verse four records they, *"Lifted up their voices and wept, till they had no more power to weep"* (NKJV). Verse 6 continues, *"Now David was greatly distressed for the people spoke of stoning him, because the soul of all the people was grieved, every man for his sons and daughters. But David strengthened himself in the Lord his God."*

The word strengthen (*khaw-zak'*) is key because it means to fasten to something to seize it and not let go.[2] Though David had lost his family, as well as hearing of possible betrayal by those who went into battle with him, it could not have been more disheartening. David went to the place of strength, which is in the secret place with God. He took off his battle gear and laid it aside and put on the Linen Ephod, which was a simple covering of a priest.

He began to present his case. Verse 8 says, *"David inquired of the Lord saying, 'Shall I pursue this troop? Shall I overtake them'"* and without fail recover all. God answered saying, *"Pursue, for you shall surely overtake them and without fail recover all"* (NKJV). The word inquire here doesn't just mean to ask questions. It is a strong word (*sha'al*) meaning to demand the rights of a citizen like one would be interrogated in a court of law.[3] Obviously, David wasn't demanding anything from God, but there is an implication he was standing on promises made that gave him certain rights. I have the sense that David entered the court of Heaven (Dan. 7:26) and wanted justice due to the enemy stealing what God had given him. David now had a sending word to pursue with.

When David came upon the Amalekites who had taken their families, he was not only to recover all that was taken from them, but also took all the spoil the Amalekites had taken in other conquests. David recovered more than what he had lost. Restoration doesn't mean making something as it had been before, but filling up what God intends for it to be.

My question to all of us is; what if David had continued to wallow in his grief and not strengthened himself, and inquired of the Lord? If he had not pursued justice, the story would be quite different. True leaders must have a redemptive mindset so that in the face of defeat one doesn't give up and accept the losses, but instead, stand on your legal rights as a redeemed citizen, enter the Court of Heaven, and find justice and recovery. I hope that by reading this book you will find the courage to go after what seemingly was lost or stolen from you and gain recovery through your redemptive rights.

THE THIEF MUST PAYBACK

Many years ago, the Lord gave me a personal promise. He said to me "I keep better books than you." I was made to understand I was to never complain about financial losses. There were times when it certainly seemed like I poured more than what was coming back in as income. Diane would always thank the Lord for it and let Him keep the books.

Recently, Diane and I were ministering at a leadership conference in Mexico City. The hosting church was very generous and accommodating. At the end of the conference, the Senior Pastor's wife told us about how they count the offerings after a meeting. She said; "we have learned we must count the offering twice because each time we do, it increases substantially." To be honest, my first thought was "you guys really have some bad counters that can't get it right the first time." Diane however heard something different. She said to the pastor's wife "we will take that as ours too." I didn't think much about it.

When we arrived at the airport in Mexico to fly home, I had exchanged some book money and their honorarium from pesos into dollars and put the dollars in my front pocket. When we arrived home that evening, I took my wallet out of my back pocket as usual, but the wallet was different. It was fat and thick, so much so I couldn't fold it. I knew how much I had in the wallet when we left and not opened my wallet for the three days we were gone. In the back of my wallet was a pad of money stuck together like a tablet bound together. They were brand new bills in sequential numbers. I was thumbing through and noticed they were all one hundred denominations. I showed Diane and she said count it. I counted it out slowly and it was fifteen one hundred dollar bills. You guessed it; Diane said, "Count it again."

With her watching closely, we counted again and it was now sixteen hundred. The final count was sixteen hundred. I was perplexed by this miracle of increase. I racked my brain as to how this happened. When I gave up trying to figure it out, the Lord reminded me of a time when we had a loss and He was keeping better books than me. We shared this story to two others and each church shared accounts that similar restitutions happened.

Exodus 22:7 says, *"If a man delivers to his neighbor money or articles to keep, and it is stolen out of the man's house, if the thief is found he shall pay double"* (NKJV). God is the righteous judge of the universe and He will give justice (Ps. 7:11). In Luke 18:7, Jesus tells a parable about an unjust judge who didn't fear God, but a widow lady who was persistent in wanting justice. The judge concluded that if he didn't render her justice she would continue to come and weary him. Jesus makes His point with this statement. *"Shall not God avenge His own elect who cry out day and night to Him, though He bears long with them?"* (NKJV). Many of us have given up before we see justice. Jesus uses this parable to reinforce the idea that though the devil is legalist, God is the just judge that has the final word. The devil does not win in the Court of Heaven.

I want to refer back to an earlier verse in Revelation 19:10 concerning the spirit of prophecy is the testimony of Jesus. In a court of law, it is necessary to have testimony to validate the claim. The Bible says that in the mouth of *"two or three witnesses let every word be established"* (2 Cor. 13:1 NKJV). The Holy Spirit will give you the spirit of prophecy to speak your case before the Lord based on the Word of God by which the redeemed have the right to speak up. Psalm 107:2 says, *"Let the redeemed of the Lord say so, whom He has redeemed from the hand of the enemy"* (NKJV). Perhaps the reason nothing has changed for you; is because you have not testified through prophesying the result of the restitution you desire. Let the redeemed speak up and speak out.

John 10:10 says, *"The thief comes only to steal and kill and destroy. I have come that they may have life, and that they may have it more abundantly"* (ESV). Notice the three ways the thief/devil comes after us.

1. The first one is to steal. This means to take resources from you that would reproduce. To demean, or to be made to feel decreased or slighted. This can happen through an offense that takes your confidence and dignity of soul. We can be made to feel uncovered or naked of soul.

2. The second one is to kill which means to take away future pro-
   ductivity and render inactive. This happens by killing our joy or
   making our service for the Lord inactive.

3. The third way the thief comes at us is to destroy. This is to
   utterly take away our identity and name. The devil will attempt
   to slander your name as to take away your influence and thus
   render you powerless.

Jesus, our Redeemer, always comes in the opposite spirit. He comes
to give life or the ability to reproduce and duplicate with multiplicity
with abundance beyond what you could do on your own. Restoration
is not one for one, but it is exponential. God redeems even times and
seasons. For instance, while in the wilderness the Hebrews began to
grumble and complain (Num. 16:32) and the ground opened up and
swallowed three thousand people. However, in Acts 2:41, after redemption came, there were three thousand who were baptized and added to
the church. The loss in one generation; God redeemed in another.

What releases people from bondage is exercising their rights as
sons and daughters of the Kingdom of God; this pushes hell back. We
have the authority on the earth to set captives free. And He wants us to
understand as children of God, we have currency stored up for us in
Heaven. There are five particular areas (discussed later in the book) that
if you function and are obedient in, you will have access into the very
throne room of God—and you'll pull into being and into place things
that you didn't know you had access to. I guarantee you will pray differently and have a totally new, exciting perspective on life.

A few years ago, I was driving to the office for a staff meeting, I
asked the Lord, "Would you give me something today that I'm going to

share with the staff because they work hard all week long, and this is the time I want to pour back into them." And the Lord said, "Son, I'm going to show you something that you will be able to apply to every problem you ever face in your life and you can deal with it." I thought, *Wow, this is like a "Get out of Jail Free" card! I need to pull over for this.* I pulled the car off to the side of the road and said, "All right, bring it on." God said, "To shrink the problem, you have to magnify the solution." Genius!

When we magnify the problem, we lose the power of the solution. When we magnify the problem more than the name of the Lord, we empower the problem, by saying (and believing) the power of the problem is greater than the power of God. Psalm 48:10 says, *"As is Your name, O God, so is Your praise to the end of the earth,"* meaning, the way we declare His name is the way the power of God is released.

One reason the enemy comes in and strikes marriages is because we magnify the faults we see in each other. Thereby we empower the spirit of division in the union. Since it was God who created marriage, then the only solution is to magnify the Lord in the marriage by honoring one another as we would honor the Lord. We have the marriage we bless or we have the marriage we curse (taken from my book, *The Power of Blessing*).

The way God redeems us is by us first repenting or acknowledging we have missed His design for marriage. Just as salvation comes through repentance, so also is the need to confess the Lord with our mouth over the marriage. Then, begin to magnify what you have that you want God to multiply in the marriage. You shrink the problem by magnifying the solution. This bond of holy matrimony only works as we operate under the covering of redemption.

Marriage doesn't work because two people have good chemistry—chemistry comes and goes. Marriages are successful because God says that a man shall leave his father and mother and be joined to his wife, that is a redemptive sign (see Gen. 2:24; Matt. 19:5; Mark 10:7; Eph. 5:31). It means God is bringing them together and He's restoring what was divided and lost in the Garden of Eden. He's restoring it in the Kingdom of God.

Adam and Eve ate the seeds of the knowledge of good and evil and became reproducers of the knowledge of evil—the kingdom of darkness. By the same token, we can eat from the Tree of Life because Jesus redeemed us. When we eat His Word and consume His thoughts, then we are reproducers of life. When you pursue a deeper understanding of these principles, the currency of Heaven is yours for entry into the Kingdom of God. There you will see the might and the power of God revealed and you can overtake and recover all that is yours.

When I was returning home from a long trip to Africa a number of years ago, I flew into JFK to board another plane to reach my destination. There I heard the Lord say, "You haven't asked for an upgrade." And I said, "Well, Lord, I'm no different from anybody else, I don't deserve any more than anybody else." He said, "You have not because you ask not." I had been flying in the "cattle car" section all week, so I said, "Lord, would you give me an upgrade?" I went up to the counter and heard a traveler angrily berating the ticket agent—a young woman probably in her early twenties. He was calling her every nasty name as she was doing the best she could to make the computer spit out what this man wanted.

I felt so grieved for her, and then heard the Holy Spirit say, "Be a father to her." So I stepped up to him, got in his face and said, "Sir, is there something I can help you with?"

"Are you an agent?"

"No, I'm more than that. I can solve your problem."

He said, "What problem? What can you do?"

"I'm a counselor," I said calmly, "and this angry, bitter spirit that you have is destroying your life. It has nothing to do with her."

He looked at me, growled, and then turned around and walked off. The ticket agent was in tears. I said, "I'm so sorry there are men like that in the world. There are some good ones, though. I'm sorry he treated you that way." I knew I had to magnify her efforts and the qualities of her service. The enemy sent someone to kill her confidence. I believe the Lord stationed me there to restore what was stolen from her that day. Through shrinking the problem of the other angry guy she gained strength and confidence again.

She said, "Thank you. This is my first day on the job and I felt paralyzed by him. I have not yet been trained how to deal with that." I told her she was doing good and her bright smile made my long trip a little brighter. "Would you like an upgrade?" She asked. "You're now sitting in seat 1A," she said.

All the way down the jetway, I was thanking God. Then when I boarded, I realized the plane was one of those small commuter flights with no first class or business seats. I was actually "upgraded" from the back of the plane to the front of the plane. But that's okay, it was a smooth flight, and I was grateful for the opportunity to shrink the attack of the enemy.

DESTROYING (GENERATIONAL CURSING) INIQUITY

Redemptive thinking allows you to pray the heart of the Father and see things from the vantage point of God's liberation and the freedom that comes with Him. Instead of magnifying or enhancing the problem, you magnify and enhance the glory of God, enlarging who He is. Then He becomes bigger than the problems. He overshadows them and destroys the iniquity of the enemy.

Romans 3:23 says, *"For all have sinned and fall short of the glory of God"* (NIV). This was the first Scripture I learned as a young boy in Sunday school. But they didn't teach me the remainder of the passage until later: *"and all are justified freely by his grace through the redemption that came by Christ Jesus. God presented Christ as a sacrifice of atonement, through the shedding of his blood—to be received by faith"* (Rom. 3:24-25 NIV).

Through the disobedience of one man, Adam, sin infected all humankind—and through the obedience of one man, Jesus, redemption embraced all humankind. Although all have sinned, Jesus the Redeemer redeemed what Adam did and He, the second Adam, restored to us what God intended from the beginning. But if we don't know that truth, we remain in bondage to whatever the enemy entraps us with. The truth is not information, but truth is a person called the Holy Spirit. Without the Spirit of Truth, we are left with only magnifying the problem and the witness of the enemy seems to be loud and often.

Now look at Ephesians 1:7, *"In him we have redemption through his blood, the forgiveness of sins, in accordance with the riches of God's grace"* (NIV). As mentioned previously, the word "redemption" simply means a ransom, to repurchase what originally belonged to the Lord. In Jesus we have redemption through His blood. His blood is currency—it is of great value that can be used in exchange for our sin.

"...in accordance with the riches of God's grace." Grace means that He redeemed us; He pardoned us when we didn't deserve it. Yet we can be pardoned and still not enjoy redemption. Grace is available, but redemption is something we have to move into; we have to choose to believe He redeemed us. Redemption not only opens the door into Heaven, but opens to reclaiming lost health and stolen wealth. People who understand the power of redemption don't feel like victims, they live like sons and daughters of the Most High God. They magnify their Father in Heaven not magnifying their self-imposed victimhood. That doesn't mean we can't approach Him with the hurts and disappointments we experience, but somewhere down the line, the revelation of how big God is must overshadow all that.

Though God wills it, the Word acknowledges it, and the Holy Spirit does it.

Father, I pray for those reading this book. May you open our eyes to see what You are wanting, us to pursue. I ask that the Holy Spirit would direct readers to abound with all that belongs to them. May we continue to recover what belongs to our spiritual estate and all our generations will see your goodness and glorify Your name. Amen!

CHAPTER 2

THE EYES OF REDEMPTION

FAITH ALWAYS LOOKS FOR potential; sin always looks for failure. When you operate in faith, you are dealing with substance. Hebrews 11:1-2 says, *"Faith is the substance of things hoped for, the evidence of things not seen. For by it the elders obtained a good Testimony"* (KJV).

Substance in the original text (*hypostasis*) means to stand under, as to have a covering.[1] Many Jewish weddings will have an archway called a Chuppah. This covering symbolizes a home or a place to belong.[2] When we talk about faith that has substance, we can see it is not about believing, but it has found a covering or a home to dwell.

Faith stands with an identity knowing your faith lies in something or someone over you. Notice that faith has evidence. The evidence is not seen, but it will stand up in the Court of Heaven. The things hoped for has been given substance or covering, so you have the right to proceed in faith. The covering that gives you the right to proceed with your claim is the covering of the name of Jesus. There is no other name in Heaven and earth whereby men can be redeemed (Acts 4:12).

Faith is standing under the redemption or covering of Christ, and He has become your dwelling place; you now have a home and faith lives there. So now we can say I have faith because I am covered by the faithful one. Galatians 2:20 says, *"Christ lives in me; and the life which I now live in the flesh I live by faith in the Son of God who loved me and gave Himself for me"* (NKJV). The reason faith has substance is that it is based on the one who bought you back from a life of fear and hopelessness. Second Corinthians 5:17 declares that *"If anyone is in Christ, he is a new creation; old things have passed away; behold, all things have become new"* (NKJV). Paul the apostle is bold in saying; we are a new species, giving us new DNA. The expectation is that we no longer are to be called faithless because we have a measure of faith that comes from dwelling with Jesus who is our Chuppah.

THE SPIRIT OF AN ORPHAN

It's not difficult to spot the orphans—especially when I am in a third world country. They are the ones with very little covering them, and you can see in their eyes the empty, hollow look. Orphans typically in those settings have no identity. They are homeless with no particular place to call home.

I saw this firsthand in Serbia, where I was taken to see many of these orphans who lived literally in a garbage dump living off the scraps of others. One little boy I remember was considered better than some because he had managed to salvage a piece of wood and some heavy duty cardboard and create a makeshift shelter.

Most orphans don't look to the future but live for the next generous handout. They hope for enough to get through until the next day, and life starts over again. I prayed for as many as would venture close to me. The filth was horrendous, but the empty feeling I got from them was worse than the smell. They have nothing to look forward to. Many do not know their family name because they were abandoned at a young age.

Many people are orphans in a spiritual sense. They carry an orphan mindset; they may be rich in the physical comforts, but they are living without a covering. They are naked when it comes to faith. They may have a New Age religious faith, but it has no substance. Jesus is the only covering for their faith.

Believing in something doesn't give you faith. If it is not covered by the blood of Jesus, it is a false sense of hope and has no eternal value. Jesus said in John 14:18, *"I will not leave you orphans; I will come to you"* (NKJV). Jesus told us in the previous verses that the Holy Spirit would be in us so we would not be empty like an orphan and we would have the identity of our Father in Heaven. Most of all we have a covering that gives us a hope and a future. A Christian who has accepted Jesus as Lord and yet complains about what they are lacking instead of using their covering to act in faith is an orphan. They are rich but live in a poverty mindset. Redemption takes you from being an orphan and renews your mind to move in the faith of the Son of God.

John 15:7 says, *"If you abide in Me, and My words abide in you, you will ask what you desire, and it shall be done for you"* (NKJV). The word abide is the connector to this verse. Abide means "to pitch your tent," and in biblical times, this was understood as putting down roots. You live where you abide. You can ask based on the Word and are you rooted. Unstable people are like nomads. They have difficulty being consistent with anything. They are inconsistent with their job, their marriage, and in serving God. They wonder why their prayers seem to go unanswered and it's because they have an orphan view of life and their prayers are uncovered. Jesus is offering them a great deal. If you will settle down and live under His covering, you will not be vulnerable to demonic contact.

Ephesians, chapter 1 verse 17 says, *"That the God of our Lord Jesus Christ, the Father of glory, may give to you a spirit of wisdom and of revelation in the knowledge of Him"* (KJV). People in the kingdom of darkness don't have the same wisdom as believers. They have "street wisdom," and children of God have Kingdom wisdom. Paul strongly urged the saints to understand how rich and glorious their inheritance is and the power they have. First Corinthians 3:19 tells us *"the wisdom of this world is foolishness to God"* (NLT). Wisdom is not having stored information about a number of topics, but in contrast, it is the application of truth. How we make application with the truth of the Word of God brings wisdom.

God asked Solomon what he wanted. Most of us would probably ask for wealth, long life, or victory over our enemies. Solomon asked for wisdom as to how to lead the people of God. Wisdom is the principle thing. One who has wisdom will never lack for anything and gives them access to many other things desired.

Many of us pray big prayers and yet prepare little for the answer to come. Without wisdom from above, the answers to some prayers would be destructive. For instance, you may ask for a million dollars to flow through your hands and yet are not prepared because you have not been faithful and responsible handling hundreds of dollars. Redemptive prayers that go unanswered are not because the answer is no, but not yet until you get wisdom to be a good steward at the level you are growing in faith for. The receiver of the gift must be equal to the size of the gift so as to contain the answer when it comes. So when we are praying redemptive prayers for lost or stolen relationships etc. are we ready for what it takes to receive such answers? I am reminded of one such example.

A mother and father had been praying for their son who had left home under angry circumstances. They grieved over the loss of their son and did all they knew to believe God for their son to come back home. One day, their son ventured to come back to visit and perhaps test the water to see it was an amiable situation. When he knocked on the door, it took the parents a minute to believe their eyes. They soon got over their shock and welcomed him in.

After a few hours of catching up, the conversation by the father soon turned from acceptance to vindication. He wanted the son to give an explanation as to why he left and had hurt them so much and why he was only thinking of himself. The son was made to feel defensive and quickly got up and left again. The sad truth is the parents had focused on the son coming back but had not prepared themselves for the event. It caught them unprepared and set the relationship back further. Redemptive praying not only is asking for wisdom but also should be preparing for when the answer comes, looks at the timing and the readiness of those seeking an answer. Are you ready for what you are pursuing? When you overtake what you were pursuing, are you prepared to recover what was lost? These parents pursued well but had not worked out forgiveness and the resentment they had for him. When it came time for them to recover their son, their hearts were not big enough to handle that big answer to their prayer. James 3:17 says, *"The wisdom that is from above is first pure, then peaceable, gentle, willing to yield, full of mercy and good fruits, without partiality and without hypocrisy"* (NKJV).

Luke 15 is a great example of the redemptive heart of Jesus. Jesus tells three parables with each one reflecting the end game of the Father, which is to redeem what was lost at the Fall of Adam. The first is a lost sheep, depicting the shepherd leaving the 99 sheep to hunt for the one lost sheep. He places the lost sheep on his shoulders and returns him to the fold. The shepherd was prepared to do what was necessary to bring the wandering lamb home.

The second parable is a lost silver coin where the story shows how the lady of the house prepared to find it. She cleaned her house so she could find the coin. In both cases, there was an effort and preparation ahead of time for when they could recover what was lost.

The third parable and perhaps the more known is of the lost son, or most of us know it as the prodigal son. This parable shows great patience on the father's part. The son, who wanted to experience life outside the covering of his father, soon discovered his vulnerability. He was still a son but was living like an orphan. His father was wealthy and had no lack, but it didn't do the prodigal any good until he returned to the covering of the father. The parable goes to great lengths to let us know the father never gave up on his son.

Redemptive thinking always causes us to seek what was lost. The father saw him a great distance away, looking beyond the sight of the natural eyes that the prophetic eyes could see him coming home. This father in the parable was ready and prepared to overtake his son and recover him. He told the servants to get the best robe, not a field hand robe but the robe of a son. He gave him his signet ring that would be equivalent to a credit card today. The father ordered a celebration for his son.

The elder brother was indignant and demanded an account for the father's actions. The elder brother was an orphan in the house because he had all the luxuries of the house but didn't know how to approach his father and thought his serving was the only part to the relationship. Both sons in a sense were prodigals. One was a prodigal of the house and the other a prodigal of the pigpen. The redemption you desire first begins with one crying out for restoration.

What do you see?

I pray the eyes of your heart may be enlightened, so that you will know what is the hope of His calling, what are the riches of the glory of His inheritance in the saints, and what is the surpassing greatness of His power toward us who believe. These are in accordance with the working of the strength of His might, which He brought about in Christ, when He raised Him from the dead and seated Him at His right hand in the heavenly places (Ephesians 1:18-20).

Paul is praying what is called an apostolic prayer. This is significant because it is a key to being able to overtake and recover your redemptive rights. Notice his prayer gives detailed instruction. He prays *"the eyes of your heart"* —not the eyes of your head—that the eyes of your understanding will capture the hope of His calling. What is the *"working of the strength of His might?"* It's the power of redemption. The riches of His glory and the riches of inheritance all operate out of the power of redemption. Here is the kicker in this verse *"the eyes of your heart may be enlightened."* The word enlighten in the original text is *phōtizō*[3] where we get our word for photograph. So it would read something like this; "I pray that the eyes of your heart may be able to take a picture of the hope that He is calling you to." The encouragement we get from this is that the Holy Spirit wants us to take a picture of what the Father has stored up for us waiting until we can steward some really big plans. If we can see it, then we can pursue them.

John 5:19 Jesus says, *"Most assuredly, I say to you, the Son can do nothing of Himself, but what He sees the Father do; for whatever He does, the Son also does in like manner"* (NKJV). Seeing with eyes of redemption comes from a place of hope and expectation. Jesus moved at the speed of revelation at what He saw His Father do. The eyes of your heart are your spirit, the eternal part of your being that sees in sync with the Holy Spirit.

We can develop the ability to see by the Spirit by first understanding our rights as one redeemed out of darkness into light. You now have light to see you are not an orphan but an inheritance beyond what you can think. Ephesians 3:20 *"Now to Him who is able to do exceedingly abundantly above all that we ask or think, according to the power that works in us"* (NKJV). Paul is letting us know we can do more than we dare to ask or beyond what we think. The next part of this verse explains it is by the power that is at work inside of us. This internal working of His power at times will be contrary to what is seen externally. Circumstances should never determine our faith level.

The power of redemption is part of the DNA God gave you when you were brought to His light. We were created with His imagination. This is not a random mind wandering around for something to grab on to. The imagination of God (read my book *The Power of Imagination*) is His thoughts toward us. We have the power to imagine or see what was meant for our lives before we were ever born.

Before I was old enough to go to school, I had a desire to one day be a preacher. While all my siblings were at school, I would gather all my sisters' dolls and Teddy bears and place them in chairs. We had a huge *Webster's Dictionary* I used for my Bible. Since I couldn't read, it didn't matter. I imagined myself preaching to my captive group. They didn't fall asleep on me, so I assumed it was a good message. I laid hands on all of them and prayed them through. I know this may seem silly now, but I was developing an imagination to see what God had placed in me before I entered this world.

YOUR BABY BOOK

Psalm 139:16 says, *"Your eyes saw my substance, being yet unformed, and in Your book they were all written; the days fashioned for me, when as yet there none of them"* (NKJV).

Just like the Lamb of God was slain before the foundation of the world, so you had things written as your potential. I call it a baby book, like young parents who have hope and vision for their child. They place things in the book and later maybe a piece of hair or first tooth. All this to say they are tracking the progress of the child. The Bible speaks of five other books that record things about us.

- Malachi 3:16, *"Then those who feared the Lord spoke to one another, and the Lord gave attention and heard it, and a book of remembrance was written before Him for those who fear the Lord and who esteem His name."*

- Psalm 87:5-6, *"And of Zion (worshippers) it will be said this one and that one were born...The Lord will record when He registers the peoples that this one was born"* (NKJV).

- Psalm 56:8, *"You number my wanderings; Put my tears into Your bottle; Are they not in your book?"* (NKJV).

- Psalm 139:16, *"My unformed substance; in your book were written"* (ESV).

- Revelation 20:15, *"And anyone not found written in the Book of Life was cast into the lake of fire"* (NKJV).

Jesus demonstrated this in Matthew 4 while confronting satan in the wilderness. Each time satan attempted to tempt Jesus to use His authority to perform; He answered with *"it is written"* three times. Jesus was referring not only to what was written from Scriptures but also what had been written before the foundation of the world that the Lamb of God (Rev. 13:8) would come and give His life to redeem those captive under satanic rule.

For me, I don't want to stand before my Father in Heaven and find the magnitude of what had been written about my potential, and I never ventured beyond the introduction of my book. Some never get beyond salvation, which is hugely important but He wants us to see our potential is not wishful thinking, but redemptive thinking. He tells us in Psalm 40:5 *"Your thoughts toward us Cannot be recounted to You in order; If I would declare and speak of them, they are more than can be numbered"* (NKJV).

TAKE CAPTIVE YOUR THOUGHTS

Second Corinthians 10:4-5 says, *"For the weapons of our warfare are not carnal but mighty in God for pulling down strongholds, casting down arguments and every high thing that exalts itself against knowledge of God, bringing every thought into captivity to the obedience of Christ"* (NKJV). We are made aware of the need to be offensive and defensive when it comes to spiritual warfare. The word warfare simply means strategy. So our strategy is not one of a natural humanistic kind. Paul the apostle is focusing the strategy toward strongholds or fortresses. The word is translated as *noema* or thoughts.[4] The stronghold is constructed out of thoughts. Thoughts of offense left unchecked can create a fortress, which blocks anything getting in and nothing getting out. Thoughts of low self-worth cause one to see from this fort in a rather skewed way. Proverbs 23:7 says as one thinks so he becomes like what he thinks.

To develop redemptive thinking, one must have a renewed mind (Rom. 12:2) that is transformative, allowing us to see beyond where they once were held captive by the thoughts of the enemy. The last part of the warfare verse is to take captive thoughts to the obedience of Christ. I know we usually think of bad thoughts that need to be taken captive, but God has thoughts for us that need to be captured and held close to our heart and numerated regularly. We should remind ourselves of all that was written about us, and the great potential that awaits those who pursue and then be prepared to overtake your rights to the possession.

Though we know we are redeemed, and our name is written in the Book of Life, my question I pose to all of us is, are we walking out all the rights and currency that Heaven says we have in the power of redemption? It's totally another realm of the Spirit. Some say, just because we have received the gift of salvation through grace doesn't mean we are fully living in the understanding of the power of redemption. If you've stepped into a redeemed life, then you're living out the power of redemption here on earth in your home and workplace—you're not waiting for something more to happen when we get to Heaven. First John 4:17 says: *"As He is, so also are we in this present world."* Because our Redeemer is alive and present, so we are in this world right now pursuing all He has purchased. Our Redeemer lives inside of us, and we carry the rights and the power of redemption. He has already redeemed everything. We are now to go after what has been redeemed but has been hidden from us by the enemy. Our Redeemer sits at the right side of God interceding for us; this tells me we carry the power to repossess what has been stolen from families.

LOOK UP YOUR REDEMPTION DRAWS NEAR

I was raised in a home where my dad worked hard at two jobs just to take care of our family of five kids. There was no extra money for anything. I never considered our family to be poor. My mother trusted God for everything and rightfully had to do so. My dad did not attend church but made sure the rest of the family went with Mom. I watched her walk out faith in the face of incredible resistance but never wavered.

During my sophomore year in high school, I announced I needed a new pair of tennis shoes. I had lettered on the senior team. All my teammates had Converse tennis shoes while I wore Keds. Everyone on the team had new rackets with Cat Gut strings; I had nylon. I felt like I stuck out like a giant wart. My mother's response was that I should pray and ask the Lord for a new pair of shoes. I thought, "Well, that's a cop-out answer. Just get it off your back and throw it onto Jesus. So now you want me to be upset with Jesus when I don't get the tennis shoes." That was my thinking at the time. I prayed a lackluster prayer asking the Lord to supply my need, and my Mom prayed too. A few weeks later, we were at Kmart buying items unrelated to my desperate need when suddenly blue lights flashed all over the building. They announced a huge sale on, you guessed it, the tennis shoes I had been asking for.

From that time on, I wanted to pray bigger prayers than just getting my wants and needs met. I was challenged to ask the Holy Spirit to show me what I should be asking for. Jesus was teaching His followers about what the end of the age to come would look like. In Luke 21:28, He said, *"When these things begin to take place, stand up and lift up your heads, because your redemption is drawing near"* (NIV). I realize Jesus was referring to His return to earth to receive His Bride, but also redemption is not only about the end of the age. Redemption is all around us all the time. When He is saying lift your heads, we can also say lift your heads now so you can see the redemptive call to pursue others who are lost without the knowledge of knowing their Redeemer.

Redemption is not only believing God for material needs, but it is also about seeing through the eyes of the Redeemer to see who He wants to set free from being an orphan to making them a son. We are part of the power of redemption. Jesus said in John 4:35, *"Lift your eyes and look at the fields, for they are already white (ripe) for harvest"* (NKJV). Having redemptive eyes will allow you to see through the eyes of your Redeemer. There is no greater joy than to see a purchased possession of Jesus being brought into the family.

BOOT CAMP FOR SERIOUS PURSUIT

Hebrews 5:14 *"Solid food belongs to those who are of full age, that is, those who by reason of use have their senses exercised to discern both good and evil"* (NKJV). Solid food is referring to the food you have to chew and when digested gives you strength. Baby food can keep you alive, but it won't build muscle. We are made skillful by reason of use.

My mother was training me to trust God for everything. If I had not had any reason to use faith, I would be a baby Christian wanting someone else to provide for me. To gain strength in the power of redemption, we will be put in situations where we must trust the Holy Spirit to guide us through. The power of God is very real and available, but if one is not skilled in how the Kingdom of God is governed if given power we would be destructive to others and ourselves.

It was 1984 and my first trip to Africa. My faith was being built for this trip, or at least I thought. I had believed for some big things to take place. I had little experience in traveling internationally. The first two weeks went well, and we saw people having encounters with the Lord. I was happy and content to finish at this level.

When it came time to fly from Kenya to Ghana, everything moved up several notches. I was refused a visa to go into Ghana. I went to the American Embassy in Nairobi. I was quickly told of some dangers of traveling into Ghana. Since I had been gone for three weeks, I was happy and eager to return home.

Sometime in the middle of the night, I awoke from a sound sleep only to sense the Holy Spirit tell me to go to Ghana. I proceeded to explain I was not allowed to enter the country. After the third time He said I was to go, I heard the Spirit say go to the airport tomorrow and go to Ghana.

In trying to be obedient, I went to the airport at my scheduled time to fly to Accra, Ghana. When I handed my ticket to the counter agent, he asked, "Where is your visa for Ghana?" I simply said, "I don't have one." It seemed to anger him, and he was quick to let me know about Americans who think they can get their way. I stepped back and said to the Holy Spirit, see this is what I was trying to explain as if He didn't know. All I heard was "Stand still and see the salvation of the Lord." There wasn't anything more I could do but stand there, looking like a lost tourist. In just a moment, two Africans got into a heated scuffle next to me. I moved out of the way, and the agent who was berating just before the fight jumped out from behind the counter attempting to break up the altercation. I saw someone motioning to me to step to the counter. A new agent had stepped up. I told him I was going to Ghana; he said rather excitedly, "The plane is here. Go now quickly and get on the plane; I will take care of your luggage." As we took off, I was praising God to see the miracle that just took place before my eyes.

As I sat there and meditated on what had just transpired, I remembered I had sent a telegram to the missionary who was to meet me telling them I was unable to come due to a visa problem. It suddenly dawned on me that no one would be there to pick me up and I have no contact information. My mind took over and raced around telling me, "You will be put in prison for illegally entering the country, and no one will know where you are." I was trying hard not to think God had tricked me into getting on this plane. I didn't realize my faith and trust were being exercised beyond what I had ever trusted Him for before.

When I arrived at the airport ready to hand them my passport vacant of a visa, suddenly behind the door, someone grabbed my arm. I thought I would leave my skin behind. I turned to see it was my missionary friend. I asked him what he was doing there. He looked surprised at what I had said. He said, "What do you mean? I am here as promised to pick you up." I said, "I sent you a telegram saying I wasn't coming." He laughed and explained his truck would not start at all the previous day, so he could not go to the post office to get the mail until that morning when the truck started.

I told him how I didn't have a visa. He took my passport and again I had to stand around like a lost tourist before I could go in. In a few minutes, he returned with my passport and a completed visa. He told me the story how a few weeks earlier the head of immigration received Christ, but it was Saturday, and he doesn't work on Saturday. However that day someone called in sick, and there was not time to replace him, so he came himself. He stamped the visa, and I was free to come into the country.

I share this long story to show how God builds our faith skill so that we will be able to step out in unknown territories and see the impossible take place. Many of you believe for miracles, and this is the reason your skill for the supernatural is being strengthened with strong food. You may feel you are being stretched to the limits, but you truly can do more than you think you can. Your spirit inside you and the Holy Spirit knows you can; now you just need to convince your mind that you can.

Let's imagine you're in school and the teacher says you can't use your phone, you can't chew gum, or talk, and if you're disrespectful, you have to stay after school. Years later, you're standing before the Supreme Court and the officer tells you there can be no phones in the courtroom, no chewing gum, no talking, and you must be respectful. If you do any of these things, you're in contempt of court and can be sent to jail. These are the exact same infractions, yet one has a greater penalty. Is that fair?

One you stay after school, the other you go to jail for doing the same thing. The difference is the authority in charge over you. We learn at all different levels at various points in our life. If we don't learn the skills when the stakes are lower, we will struggle in life when it could affect us for decades to come.

HE PREPARES A TABLE FOR ME

Psalm 23 (NKJV) is an interesting picture of a shepherd depicted as Jesus, the Great Shepherd, leading His sheep up through the passages and crevices of the rocks. I want to lay out for us the lessons in a chronology that seems to be important to the progression toward the ultimate place of maturity.

Lesson 1. You *"shall not want."* This doesn't mean you have no needs or desires, only trusting for everything.

Lesson 2. *"He makes me lie down…"* Not only is this for rest, but we need to learn to listen in case He says "get down." It may just be I have to learn to duck due to the place we are going.

Lesson 3. *"He leads me beside still waters."* Going higher with Him will require learning how to drink from Him and finding places of rest for the next assignment.

Lesson 4. *"He restores my soul."* The soul being the mind, will, and intellect needs restoring. Most moral failures come from being over-taxed and emotionally depleted. Learning how to receive emotional refueling is crucial for the altitude He is taking you.

Lesson 5. He leads through paths that are always in right relations with Him. He never would lead you into any venture that would cause separate paths from Him.

Lesson 6. While He is leading and there appears a threat like wolves hanging over the cliffs casting their shadow on the sheep; remember, He carries a rod that will deal a deadly blow to the wolves and a staff that will pull any sheep out of harm's way. This lesson is the most difficult for most because it deals with trust while circumstances surrounding you are screaming out its options of attack.

Lesson 7. The last lesson is the target for this journey. He prepares a table for you in the presence of your enemies. My picture is of the table being at the top of the mountain. There we have learned trust and not to fear enough to eat while our enemies are glaring at us. Nothing annoys the devil any more than to eat in front of him. When he finds out, you will not be disrupted or dissuaded, and you will not lose your appetite because the Shepherd of your soul is there.

Though we carry the power of redemption inside, we have to grow into the faith of the Redeemer to pull out of the enemy's hands what belongs to us. The enemy doesn't let go until he knows you are confident of your rights as one who is redeemed and one who is now redeeming.

Galatians 4:1-2 *"Now, I say that the heir, as long as he is a child, does not differ at all from a slave, though he is master of all, but is under guardians and stewards until the time appointed by the father"* (NKJV). This should answer the question for some of us as to why we are not seeing our redemptive rights working on our behalf. The word picture Paul gives is the promise to the heir is huge, and he is in line for the inheritance. In Jewish culture, the father determines the maturity of the son before he is released into his fullness.

You might not be seeing what you have an expectation for at the moment—which only means you are being groomed to fit the size of the inheritance. The foundation determines the height of the structure. It seems to take longer to dig and certify the foundation more than any other part of the building.

What happens in the secret moments of the heart are not seen publicly, but it is still as much of the building as what is seen in front of people. The longevity of the inheritance or ministry is tied directly to the depth of character that was forged in the times of testing. Do not despise or resent the time you have been placed under tutors and stewards because it will be worth the time of internal building to see the strength of the person once they are released by their father. We all need spiritual mothers and fathers in our tutorial process. How we handle submitting to those who genuinely love us will expedite the time needed to learn the lesson of humility and serving. In John 14:2, Jesus uses this same illustration in this passage: *"In My Father's house are many mansions (places/rooms) if it were not so, I would have told you. I go to prepare a place for you"* (NKJV).

Every Jewish young man understood what Jesus was saying. In a wealthy family, homes were built inside what we would call today a family compound. When a young man would take a bride, he would extend a cup of wine to her. If she drank from the cup and then he would drink from the same cup, it meant they were engaged or betrothed. The young man would leave and begin building their home inside the family estate or compound. The father was in charge of determining when the building was complete before the son could return and take his bride to his new home. Jesus said in Matthew 24:36, *"But of that day and hour no one knows, not even the angels of heaven, but My Father only"* (NKJV). Though you feel you have been waiting long to see a breakthrough for your time of coming above ground level, just know preparations are happening on your behalf because you have redemption rights to what has been promised.

I know most of us think of John 14:2 as referring to our Mansion in Glory. In many Scriptures, there is a duality of thought. One thought is not better than another; the only difference is in the application. I suggest this verse could also apply to the present. The word mansion was not the best translation of this description. Many translate this, as *"in My Father's House there are many rooms or places."* Since we know we have been called the temple of God and the House of God in Scripture, then consider this thought; in you the house of God, there are many rooms. Perhaps the Holy Spirit wants to fill many places inside you. Some rooms may have posted signs on the door like, "do not enter; private." Part of preparing us to reign in full redemption rights is to allow the inspector to enter every room and decorate, as He knows the Father would want.

In Luke 19:44, Jesus is foretelling of the destruction of the Temple. He uses a phrase that is appropriate to this subject. *"You did not recognize the time of your visitation."* This word visitation has significant meaning even more so in the original Greek. It *(episkopē)* means to inspect.[5] Jesus was saying I came to you for inspection and you were not aware of it or even ready for it. The great thing about when the Holy Spirit inspects, it is never for failure, but to prepare or make ready for occupancy. A visitation from the Lord today is not only about a special revival taking place, but also inspecting our hearts to see if we are ready to handle the weightiness of His Presence to come. He is using every possible means necessary to not fail us in the inspection but sign off on the next phase of building a habitation for Himself. The promises of the Lord are yes and Amen; He has not changed His mind about fulfilling your redemption.

KEEP THE PROMISE ALIVE IN YOU

The Book of Jeremiah gives us a great picture of what redemptive thinking looks like:

Now I want to say something more about this city. You have been saying, "It will fall to the king of Babylon through war, famine, and disease." But this is what the Lord, the God of Israel, says: I will certainly bring my people back again from all the countries where I will scatter them in my fury. I will bring them back to this very city and let them live in peace and safety. They will be my people, and I will be their God. And I will give them one heart and one purpose: to worship me forever, for their own good and for the good of all their descendants. And I will make an everlasting covenant with them: I will never stop doing good for them. I will put a desire in their hearts to worship me, and they will never leave me. I will find joy doing good for them and will faithfully and wholeheartedly replant them in this land. ... Fields will again be bought and sold in this land about which you now say, "It has been ravaged by the Babylonians, a desolate land where people and animals have all disappeared." Yes, fields will once again be bought and sold—deeds signed and sealed and witnessed—in the land of Benjamin and here in Jerusalem, in the towns of Judah and in the hill country, in the foothills of Judah and in the Negev, too. For someday I will restore prosperity to them; I, the Lord, have spoken (Jeremiah 32:36-41;43-44 NLT).

The Word of the Lord came to Jeremiah to redeem the land that was in his uncle's family. Jeremiah had the right of redemption according to Jewish Law. He could either pass it up and then it would be up to someone else in the family to claim the right.

The interesting part about this story is Jeremiah is in prison for prophesying Babylon would take the city. The question is; why would you buy land when you believe the city would be captured. Though Jeremiah had the rights to the land to buy, he had to determine if it was a good deal in light of the coming doom. This is a prophetic picture of how redemption is seen in God's eyes. He wanted Jeremiah to keep his prophetic future alive by investing into what would be restored. While everyone wants to sell and get out of town, Jeremiah sees God is going to restore the city eventually. Through Jeremiah buying the land, he was staking his claim on his redemptive rights to the family legacy.

I read about a pastor in a small town in the mountains of California who was struggling to find a breakthrough in the church there. He felt it was the worst place in the world you ever would want to pastor. One day while asking the Lord for an understanding of why they did not see any fruit there, the Lord spoke to his heart; "Until you love the city, you can't pastor the city." God told him to go out and buy a cemetery plot and plan to live his days there. The pastor told God, "I don't want to be buried here, I don't even want to stay here, much less be buried here." And God said, "Until you learn to live and love this place and its people, you have no power and authority in here." When he finally did what God told him to do, revival hit that little town. Because he was obedient and bought land, choosing to put down roots there, God could use him mightily. When he made a commitment and was connected to the land, God recovered the area for Himself.

It may be that God will speak to your heart how you are to invest in what you want to see redeemed. It's easy to pray about claiming your redemptive possessions, but when the Holy Spirit is prompting you, it's time to "put some skin in the game," then you know He is getting ready to tie up loose ends and connect you to your claim. God so loved the world He redeemed the world with His best investment of love, His Son. I am not saying we can buy anything from God, but there are times we are to act in faith toward what we are to believe for.

Pray this with me. Father, I ask that You would give us redemptive eyes to see the end from the beginning. Help us all to keep alive the promises of reclaiming all that You have given to us to oversee. You made us caretakers of our garden, and we want to be faithful to guard and keep pure our legacy for the next generation who will follow us.

May the Lord bless you with favor to prosper and be in health so you may have the fullness of life to see your proclamation become a fully realized claim to your inheritance.

CHAPTER 3

TAKING DOMINION OVER CREATION

THE STORY OF CREATION was one of trust. Could God trust man/ Adam to take dominion over the creation of God? Adam was given everything necessary to do the job. He was given instruction for his job in The Garden. He had complete authority and whatever Adam named the animals that became their names. The instruction to take dominion means to govern or rule. Adam had God's support; he had God's presence.

He knew the one thing that would cause him to be unsuccessful and separate from the ability to govern was the Tree of Good and Evil. Adam probably wasn't sure why this tree was off limits because all the other trees were good. Why this one? The one thing Adam had not been schooled on was that evil was not just about a tree, but a fallen prince looking for a way to gain authority over God's creation again.

When another voice or thought was introduced into The Garden, everything changed. What once was pure had been corrupted, thus the need for redemption and to buy back the rights to creation. What Adam gave away through his authority or right to sin or overcome sin, was all laid on him. Adam was found not to be trusted, so the battle over who we are began.

The right to creation has been redeemed, but the battle continues with lies about our redemption. Though the price has been paid, it comes back once again to trust our Redeemer, so we can fully take dominion once again.

THE STORY UNFOLDS

"Neither wild plants nor grains were growing on the earth. For the Lord God had not yet sent rain to water the earth, and there were no people to cultivate the soil" (Gen. 2:5 NLT).

Genesis is the history of the heavens and the earth. This particular verse reveals that before any plant, herb, or grains of the field was in the earth, nothing was going on, and nothing was growing. *"For the Lord God had not yet caused it to rain on the earth, as there was no one to till the ground."* In other words, God was not going to release rain until there was someone there to cultivate it.

The word "cultivate" means to bring to full potential. It is the same word for men that God uses in the Bible as husband, husbandry, or husbandman. The word itself means a grower.[1] A husband is to grow his wife and family into the image of God. Husbands are to encourage, support, and bless the family so they can come into the full potential God called them to.

Notice God did not release multiplication on the earth until after there was someone to care for The Garden. If we are praying prayers of multiplication, but we're not ready to take care of what He multiplies to, it will be static and not increase. For example, if we're not prepared and ready to give back to the Lord and honor Him with our substance, we're not ready to cultivate or grow what we already have—yet we're praying and believing God for financial miracles, it's not going to happen. Some get disappointed when they don't see an increase, and that is due to not understanding the principle of sowing and reaping.

Look at verse 6, *"But a mist went up from the earth and watered the whole face of the ground (NKJV)."* No rain had fallen from the heavens at that point. Instead, water came up as a mist from the ground.

"And the Lord God formed man of the dust of the ground, and breathed into his nostrils the breath of life; and man became a living being" (Gen. 2:7 NKJV). The Lord God formed the man's physical body from dirt, and He breathed into man the breath of God. At that moment, man came to life not because of coming from an earthen substance, but because of the Spirit of God or seed from another world. Adam now possessed natural and supernatural qualities. The Bible describes Adam as a living being. The best translation, says that man became a speaking spirit.

Man was now a three-part being. This intimate, loving action by God is what causes us to be separated from the rest of creation. All other animals carry a body and soul but not the Spirit of God. Adam now being a body possessing a mind—a spirit with superior qualities over the rest of creation. Most of all we became a speaking spirit. This gave us the ability to speak over our family/garden words of life that causes people to grow.

Before the Fall, Adam and Eve were dominated by their spirit. After the Fall, it all flipped. Man became ruled by his mind, which was the result of eating from the tree of knowledge. Before they lost their position in paradise, the first couple saw life through the filter of God's glory that had been covering their bodies. Adam would look at Eve through glory, and she would see him as the wonderful creation of God. When they gave up their rights to rule, they lost the covering of God. Adam and Eve saw each other for the first time outside of God's glorious covering.

The first thing they did was to blame one another. Adam blamed God for the woman He gave him. The woman blamed the devil; who deceived her. It's easy to now see without living a life of redemption; we tend to blame one another. When the glory departs, all we can see is one another's nakedness. A fault-finding spirit doesn't come through eyes of redemption, but through eyes that have yet to understand their place of rule.

God breathed life and likeness into us. He put something of Himself inside us so we would be divinely connected with Him. When we pray, it's not a physical body out of dust that's praying; it is our spiritual nature that prays to Him. Psalm 42:7 says, *"Deep calls to deep...."* (NIV). Our spirit is praying.

Romans 8:26 says, *"In the same way the Spirit also helps our weakness; for we do not know how to pray as we should, but the Spirit Himself intercedes for us with groaning too deep for words."* When we don't know what to pray for as we should, the Spirit is in us, praying through us with a language of Heaven. Since man became dominated by his intellect; through redemption, we were given the language of the Spirit to pray beyond our mental capabilities. Since the redemption through a new covenant, we again have divine contact with our Creator. We are taking back our place to rule and have dominion.

WE ARE CALLED TO PROCREATE

Typically, the word procreate means to regenerate or have babies. In this context, it is two words: pro meaning to advance something, and create meaning to make something that wasn't seen before. In a similar way, Paul told us we can have the same faith as Abraham in Romans 4:17, *"God who gives life to the dead and calls those things which do not exist as though they did"* (NKJV).

I call this procreating by being a partner with the Holy Spirit as a speaking spirit to speak life to things, which do not exist by natural senses as though they do exist. Being a redemptive partner with Christ is a procreator. By the way, we are, after all, a speaking spirit called to step into The Garden, so it can begin to rain, and we can see our garden grow. We know God does not change His mind about what He created, so what was originally intended is now restored back to the place of the Redeemed of the Lord to pick up the role again as a partner in creation.

Hebrews 1:2-3 says, *"In the last days (God) has spoken to us by His Son, whom He has appointed heir of all things, through whom also He made the worlds; who being the brightness of His glory and the express image of His person, and upholding all things by the word of is power, when He had by Himself purged our sins, sat down at the right hand of the Majesty on high"* (NKJV). This gives us a glimpse into how we can become part of this glory of procreation. The writer of Hebrews starts by declaring that since the new covenant, God speaks to us through our Redeemer, Jesus Christ, through whom He made the worlds. Hebrews also describes Jesus as the expression of the image of His person. The word person can be broken down into two words: per meaning to pass through, and son meaning sound where we get the word sonic from. Together, person means the sound that passes through.

So let's put all the pieces together in this one sentence. Jesus, in these last days, is speaking to us as an expression of the sound of God passing through Him. Let's now see this through the light of redemption. Those who He has redeemed have become His person; whose sound now passes through us. Again because we are a speaking spirit and become procreators with Him, it's not unusual for His word to pass through us to speak over our garden of oversight.

Now the spirit of prophecy takes on more significance. We are a speaking spirit that speaks prophetically over what He has given us redemptive dominion over. This is how we procreate our garden; through speaking life over what was once under the control of the serpent. In the same way, God spoke to the first creation and said, *"Let there be,"* we can also as the redeemed co-creators speak life because He originally set all things into existence. Now we are calling our garden back into the original intention of God before the Fall of Adam. Dead things don't reproduce—only things alive. He has redeemed us from death and quickened us to sit with Him in heavenly places (Eph. 2:6-7). Sitting with Him in that position as a procreator is the best vantage point to rule from.

THE POWER OF LIFE AND DEATH

Proverbs 18:21 says, *"Death and life are in the power of the tongue, and those who love it will eat its fruit"* (NKJV).

Just like Adam was given the necessary authority and tools to either fail or succeed, so we too are given what we need to fail or succeed. God challenged Israel before they entered their Land of Promise. He told them if they chose life and blessing, they would prosper and be successful in the land, but if they chose death and cursing, they would find decrease and opposition from their enemies.

God has given us the same admonishment to bless and not curse. Blessing is speaking life over something to be as God intended. Cursing is speaking deadly things by only saying how they appear at the moment. God did not call us to report how things around us are at the moment like a television news report. We are called to speak those things that are not as though they are to be. When we use words of life, creative blessings follow after us.

Where once defeated, we now win simply by changing our language from earthly to heavenly. Jesus said in John 6:63: *"The words that I speak to you are spirit and they are life"* (NKJV). When He spoke those words, over five hundred followers left Him that day because they were offended at what they heard. Because they did not hear with spiritual discernment, they did not understand He was speaking in supernatural terms. They were on an FM Frequency, and Jesus was on World Wide Satellite.

John 1:1-3 tells us, *"In the beginning was the Word and the Word was with God and the Word was God. He [Word] was in the beginning with God. All things were made through Him, [Word] and without Him [Word] nothing was made that was made"* (NKJV). It is key to understand the power of redemption is connected to this passage. All of creation came about as the result of the Word. Notice Word is capitalized to show a person, not the Bible. Jesus, our Redeemer, is also called the Word of God and was present and involved with creation. The take away I want us to see from this is nothing happened creatively without the Word.

For us to function as part of the anointing of redemption, we must see the Word was in the beginning calling chaos into order, or better still, calling the unformed into formation (Gen. 1:2). Chaos lives and exists in darkness when the Word speaks over darkness; light/revelation consumes the darkness as powerless. Everything came to order or into design. Adam was placed in this order to keep the order. While in this order, creation flourished and multiplied.

Only when another voice entered in, did the order become divided through listening to another. Lucifer cannot create anything but only disrupt and corrupt the created design of God. When the corruption was finalized through the obedience of the outside suggestion to eat of the forbidden, chaos entered once again. It wasn't at the level of creation, but it was aimed at the very creation God had invested His own spirit into—which was Adam. The serpent knows Adam perhaps may not fall for such a blatant assault against God, so the serpent gets Adam's wife's attention with all the benefits of disobedience. My point being, the devil wants to corrupt what God has created in all of us and sometimes uses means and people we felt safe with to bring disorder into our garden to disrupt the glory God placed there.

I hope we can see the need for our Redeemer was not just to rescue us, but to restore us to the original design and flourish under His order. If we are to be co-creators, we also must use the Word of God.

Nothing that was created was made without the Word. If the Word was needed in the beginning, then it's also needed today to restore us to His design. Psalm 107:20, says *"He sent His word and healed them, and delivered them from their destructions"* (NKJV). It was the word sent that brought about restoring of health. Notice in this passage, word was not capitalized. This was before Jesus came as Redeemer. Now, His

Word is not an old covenant, but alive backed up by the power of resurrection. John 1:14 goes further to explain, *"And the Word became flesh and dwelt among us, and we beheld His glory, the glory as of the only begotten of the Father, full of grace and truth"* (NKJV). The Word that was at creation took on the form of a man (Phil. 2:7) to transfer the same spirit to us that was in the beginning that destroyed chaos and brought creative order.

In John 14:17, we read: *"The Spirit of Truth, whom the world cannot receive, because it neither sees Him nor knows Him; but you know Him, for He dwells with you and will be in you"* (NKJV). After the resurrection, the Holy Spirit moved from being with them to being inside of them. The Spirit of Truth present at creation has now moved inside of you and me to guide us as procreators. Nothing was created without the Word, and now the one who guides and reminds (John 14:25) us of everything our Redeemer the Word said is now living inside us. How cool is that? It's more than cool; it's powerful and creative.

Notice both Genesis 1:1 and John 1:1 start by saying *"in the beginning"* and have similar meanings referring to the head or the first fruit. So, what was the first or first fruit? In the beginning, the first fruit was the Word. Romans 8:29 speaks of Jesus as the firstborn among many brethren. Let's tie this together by saying; anything created that has the power to dislodge chaotic darkness must begin with the beginning/ Word; for it to be an established order.

Allow me one last thought about the Word at creation. Genesis 1:2 describes the chaos on the earth with water covering the whole earth and darkness on the face of the deep, but notice what happens; the Spirit of God was hovering/brooding over the face of the waters. The meaning of brooding is the idea of inseminating. The Holy Spirit was injecting the Word into creation so it would be conformed to the intention of the Word. The term word is also what we call "seed" (Greek/sperma) in which the Spirit of Truth was seeding the darkness, and the darkness was destroyed when God spoke. The Word and the Spirit always work in tandem to bring about God's order. The first thing God confronts in creation is the darkness. God spoke for light to come and so it was. We don't see the sun and moon created until verse 14. I think when God said *"let there be light,"* He was not speaking about the sun; He spoke to Himself and exposed darkness to the radiance of His glory.

First John 4:4 says, *"Greater is He who is in you than he that is in the world"* (KJV). The greater light, the greater word, and the greater power live in us to take dominion over The Garden you have been called to steward. First Peter 4:10 says, *"As each one has received a gift, minister it to another, as good stewards of the manifold grace of God"* (NKJV). The word stewarding is not used much these days, but the same idea shows up in words such as manager or overseer. The original (*oikonomos*) means to be a caretaker of the wealth of another.[2] The concept is more than just a job of being in charge; it is to be seen as taking care something as if it were your own, while keeping in mind there is accountability overseeing you.

Jesus illustrated this dynamic in the parables; especially regarding the talents in Matthew 25:14. Jesus makes a point up front to say this parable is concerning the Kingdom of Heaven which is how the accountability of stewardship functions. I think this parable could have easily been called the parable of trust. The first lesson of this story is seen in verse 15. He gave them each a measured weight of money called a talent according to their ability. What ability do you think the owner was looking for in each of the servants? Perhaps it was based on past experience with these three different workers, or maybe it was based on their different types of personality, or most likely it was their relationship to him. Since this is a parable, we can't say for sure because parables have many applications.

The reason I say relationship is based on the worker who received one talent. When the owner returned, he wanted an accounting of how they invested his money and to see what the increase was. The person who received one talent immediately dug a hole and buried it. Here is the explanation of his thinking recorded in verses 24-25. He said, *"I know you to be a hard man reaping where you have not sown and gathering where you have not scattered seed. And I was afraid, and went and hid your talent in the ground. Look, there you have what is yours"* (NKJV).

The fallacy was the servant thought he really knew the owner, but clearly, if he had, he would have known the owner expected him to do something with what had been given him. If he had really known the master, he also would have known he gives rewards for faithfulness and trust. The other two received an upgrade in authority to rule over greater things. The guy who only had the one lost what he had. In my imagination, I think had the servant invested the talent and lost it in the investment he would have had at least shown faith by trying to go for it. The only penalty was for nothing.

Being thankful for redemption is admirable, but if we truly value what our Redeemer did, we would want to partner with Him for greater fruit. The kingdom example is to join in seeking the lost which was the original purpose for His sacrifice. Since this was an example how the Kingdom of God works, then we can conclude there is an expectation of our stewardship for the gifts of redemption we have been given. If we are asking for an increase in influence or even financially, we can use this as criteria of our trust ability, are we investors in the kingdom or one who hides from the risks one faces when they move forward in the Kingdom of God?

To further illustrate this point, look at what Jesus said in John 4:10. While Jesus was waiting for the disciples to bring Him something to eat, He purposely waited by a well that would normally be a center of a town since water was essential to the life of a community. A woman of Samaria came to the well alone, probably by later descriptions she was cast out by the rest of the women who would come together to visit and draw water for their families. Jesus talking to a woman who was not a Jew was probably stepping over traditional barriers. After discussing the water topic, the depth of the well, and that Jesus did not bring anything to draw water with; He says to her *"If you knew the gift of God and who it is who says to you, 'Give Me a drink,' you would have asked Him and He would have given you living water"* (John 4:10 NKJV).

The reason the woman didn't ask for this living water was that she did not know Him any way other than as just another Jew who would reject her and treat her with shame. Just like the servant who hid the talent thinking he really knew the owner, we tend to see people through our experiences and react the way we would in similar circumstances. The point I am attempting to make is how much we need to be aware that redemption is not for the sole purpose of going to Heaven one day, but that until that time, we will bury our potential given to us for the purpose of partnering in redemption. If I truly intimately knew the giver of such a marvelous gift, I would be asking for an understanding how to be a more faithful steward of the Word and Spirit.

A young woman approached me one day and said, "I want you to pray that I'll get another car."

I said to her "I thought you had a car?"

"Well, I did, but I gave it away."

"Why did you give it away?"

"Because I read the testimony of how a famous televangelist had given his car away and God gave him two cars better than the one he gave away."

"Ok then what is the problem, you should have at least one new car."

"I am waiting for God to give me my car."

"I don't need to pray for you since you are waiting for your car."

She soon figured out her assumption was not a word from God, but a testimony of someone else. She wanted the gift someone else received as a result of hearing and obeying without any intimate communication with one who can make these things possible. If she knew the gift of God, she would have known He wants to have fellowship, and from that comes words of instruction. God so loved the world that He gave the gift of His Son (John 3:16). The gift we need to know is not the gift of a new car, but the gift of redemption. From the gift of redemption comes rewards and wonderful benefits, but we shouldn't think for a moment that these benefits come by taking shortcuts around the giver of these blessings. This young woman eventually went back into debt to buy another car because she missed the best part of these kinds of miracles—the encounters she could have received while waiting for a specific word about her car. We have to be not only speaking spirits but listening spirits as well.

ENFORCING THE JUDGMENTS WRITTEN

I have a friend who is a paralegal and quite good at what she does. One area of her expertise is to help people receive proceeds that have been handed down by courts. In many cases, the clients don't receive what was decreed. For instance, a client may receive a favorable verdict for a financial settlement. The person may rejoice in the favorable verdict, but months and years later never see a dime of the judgment. My friend either reminds the loser in the case of the verdict to pay. They can be taken back to court and shown they are in contempt of court and the penalty is increased. They can lose property or other assets for failure to abide by the ruling.

Daniel 7:21-22 says, *"I was watching and the same horn was making war with the saints, and prevailing against them, until the Ancient of Days came, and a judgment was made in favor of the saints of the Most High, and the time came for to possess the kingdom"* (NKJV).

In the same way, we are recipients of the most favorable decree handed down by the Judge of the universe. Our enemy refuses to give up ground until the victory that came from the cross and resurrection is enforced. Many Christians can recite what the word says they can expect in their new life of freedom, but continue to live as if it is a nice story that doesn't work for them. The devil knows he is defeated, but will only give up what Jesus purchased when forced to do so.

There are spiritual ways we will discuss in the coming chapter to make the deceiver give back what has already been decreed as yours. You have a legal right to go before the Court of Heaven and demand the thief lets go of what the Lamb of God has purchased. We know He has purchased a bride and the power of redemption for the Bride of Christ is all powerful.

Daniel 9:2; *"In the first year of his reign (Darius) I, Daniel, understood by the books the number of the years specified by the word of the Lord through Jeremiah the prophet, that He would accomplish seventy years in the desolations of Jerusalem"* (NKJV).

Daniel was reading the scrolls of Jeremiah about the 70 years of captivity and the destruction of Jerusalem. Daniel realized the 70 years had been completed, but nothing had changed. This is a prime example of how we can read about our victory in Scripture, but not everyone is living in that reality. Daniel proceeded by prayer and fasting for three weeks to find what the missing element was for the return of the people to the land. In Daniel 10:12, the angel comes to Daniel saying: *"From the first day that you set your heart to understand, and to humble yourself before your God, your words were heard; and I have come because of your words"* (NKJV).

It is important to note that nothing was happening or going to happen until Daniel set his heart on reconciling what was decreed about the 70 years of captivity and why nothing was changing though the sentence had been fulfilled. As you read on further in chapter 10, you discover the ruling prince of darkness over Persia had held on to the captivity and was continuing to exact captivity rule over them even though God had decreed they were free. We will stay in the slavery we accept until our heart is set on getting out from under the domain that has held us captive.

I know of people who have had wonderful promises spoken over their lives by prophecy or reading of the promises in the word only later to become discouraged because they have not seen the fulfillment of those words. There may be a variety of reasons why there was a performance of what they were expecting. I will mention two factors.

When we receive something we consider to be born of the Spirit, we immediately should act as Daniel and start praying for the word to come fully. Too many people think that a word from the Lord is an automatic mandate like a "get out of jail free card." Most words are opportunities to partner with that word for it to come to pass. There are prophetic words conditional upon one's response and obedience. Listen to the word reread from time to time because you will hear differently as you grow into that word.

Many years ago when I was first starting out as a pastor, I was asked to officiate a funeral service. As I was standing next to the widow viewing the body of her husband, she leaned over to me and said; "He died before his time." The man was obviously up in years at least from the vantage point of a 24-year-old. Not having much experience at that time with such a question, I asked her why she thought he died before his time. She looked at me as if I should know. I suppose my somewhat young inexperienced puzzled look surprised her. She eventually said, "He died with unfulfilled prophetic words." From what I learned later of the man, he was one to rarely attend church and giving was more like restaurant tipping. The truth is we must claim it and proclaim it.

The second factor can be the word never got planted in your heart. When the angel Gabriel announced to Mary she was going to have a son; her first thought was "how could this be because I have never been intimate with a man?" To her credit, not understanding how this could naturally happen she responded to Gabriel; *"May it be done to me according to your word"* (Luke 1:38). When she accepted the opportunity to be a part of the miracle of the word instead of being a spectator, it went well for her.

I hear this phrase when someone is not sure if they believe the word that came to them or not, they will say; "put it on the shelf." The problem with this cute cliché is it is not biblical. I have never read in Scripture where there is a prophetic shelf to store prophetic words. If it doesn't set a fire off inside you like life just moved in, then don't shelve it, trash it. A word you put on the shelf that you do not plant in you, won't grow— even if it is a true word.

In Haggai 2:19, the question is posed to those who were being corrected by the prophet; *"Is the seed still in the barn?"* (NKJV). The picture here is humorous to me because there are those who hear the word but never plant it since they don't see it as a seed from the Kingdom of God and they just sit on it, put it on the prophetic shelf in the barn, and forget about it. When things are not going too well, just remember; oh yeah I forgot to plant it—like the lady who thought if God said it, then her husband didn't need to do anything. Contrary to that thought, we must become partners with the Spirit to keep that word alive in our heart.

First Timothy 1:18 says, *"This charge I commit to you, son Timothy, according to the prophecies previously made concerning you, that by them you may wage the good warfare"* (NKJV). The seasoned apostle Paul is giving sound advice to his young son in the faith starting his life in ministry. Paul tells him to use the prophetic words given by the elders as a weapon to wage warfare. Warfare means strategy. In essence, Paul is teaching this young man that to be successful, use what God has spoken over your life as ammunition against the enemy to enforce the victory given to you as one having rights as a citizen of a powerful country.

When I first moved to Tyler, Texas, I was not sure of all that would happen, but I knew one thing for sure—God had sent me. I had particular words of promise conditional upon me fulfilling my role as a leader. Soon after I arrived, there was a medical need for one of my kids. It looked like surgery was imminent. The night before the surgery was to take place; I went into the room where my baby was so sick. I reminded the Lord of the word He said to me if I would come. It was a word about being my healer and provider. The next morning we took our daughter to the hospital for the ear surgery, and all the way there, I kept declaring to God, *I am here because you sent me and now I am here at this hospital which is not your will.* I was a young father scared for my baby and yet confused about what was happening. A few minutes after the nurse took her for surgical prep, she returned and asked if this was the same baby they had examined the day before. Now I was really confused. Thirty minutes later they brought her out and placed her in my arms and said they couldn't find anything wrong with her. I am convinced had I not used the weapons I was given of personal words to me; we would have had surgery that day. Though God had given me precious promises to stand on, it was up to me to enforce the victory decreed over my life.

There may be financial decrees made on behalf of you and your family but it is up to you to wrangle it out of the hands of the evil one.

Lord Jesus, we thank You for being the breaker that has allowed us to enter into a glorious freedom. I pray we know the power that has been invested in all the redeemed ones. Today, our prayer is that we would have new strategies to enforce the victory You purchased for us. Right now would You give the readers of this book promises they can go to war with and that will become their intercessory ammunition? From this day forward, we stand on what You have already done, and we insist on the freedom of Heaven come to earth. Let faith propel us into a fresh dimension to see the life we now live, through the eyes of the redeemed. Amen!

CHAPTER 4

THE FIRST AND LAST WAR

WE READ IN REVELATION 12:7 that *"War broke out in heaven: Michael and his angels fought with the dragon; and the dragon and his angels fought, but they did not prevail, nor was a place found for them in heaven any longer"* (NKJV).

The very reason we needed to be redeemed began with a war in Heaven. The dragon, also called lucifer, was a created high-ranking angel that was to oversee worship around the throne of God. Isaiah 14:12 names him as lucifer as one who was in the throne room and was cast down to earth, a planet of darkness. Lucifer fell from being an angel of light to being called the prince of darkness. Notice the wording that describes the dragon as losing its place in Heaven.

Ephesians 4:27 admonishes us not to *"give place to the devil"* (NKJV). The reason two writers repeat this in Scripture is that it is exactly what the devil wants to do today. The enemy of your soul wants to find a place or foothold so he can bring mixture and bring a hybrid thinking to those who were redeemed from him having a place in their lives.

Let me bring you back to Genesis to the promise God gave to the seed of the woman. Genesis 3:15 says the seed of the woman *"will crush your head and you will strike His heel"* (NIV). The seed of the woman refers to Jesus who was born of a woman to crush the headship and rule of the serpent. It excites me to think the seed of the woman, Jesus, became the seed we are born again from. In short, we now carry the same seed that continues to crush the devil and his angels on earth. The serpent was cursed and reduced to slither on the ground. The serpent represents the devil's attempt to find an inroad to our families. I hope you now see you have the power of redemption to crush every temptation or any attack against the property of Christ.

In John 14:30, Jesus tells his disciples, *"The ruler of this world is coming, and has nothing in Me"* (NKJV). Wow! Jesus just gave us a huge clue how the devil gets a foothold over people. The devil goes about like a hungry lion looking for openings to take advantage of his prey. The devil listens for a resonating sound (we will discuss later in this chapter), so he can connect with the same sound. When Jesus was in the Garden of Gethsemane, the Roman soldiers came asking for Him. Each time Jesus answered *"I am He"* and each time He answered them, they fell to the ground. The soldiers could not take Him because there was nothing in Jesus that resonated or agreed with the same spirit they were of. Jesus had to allow them to take Him physically to fulfill His purpose of dying for us.

Romans 16:20 says, *"And the God of peace will crush Satan under your feet shortly"* (NKJV). We were given the same promise to crush the serpent as was spoken about the seed of the woman. In the same context, Jesus instructs His disciples in Matthew 10:14 that if they go into a city and do not receive you there, shake the dust off your feet as a testimony against them. Part of the curse placed on the serpent by God in Genesis was that he would go on the ground and eat the dust. Here is the connection. If we don't get rid of the dust of offenses that comes through rejection and various forms of not being accepted, then the serpent will eat the dust and continue to feed off the offense. The dust of an unresolved issue can result in the serpent gaining a place in our thinking and default reactions. Dealing with the small issues at the moment keeps our feet clear of the dust of hurts that attracts familiar demonic spirits.

One principle of life is everything that lives must be fed. A demon is a disembodied spirit looking for a host home. For instance, a spirit of fear is attracted to those who exhibit fear. It is like devil's food cake. They are supported by behavior that is the opposite of how the kingdom rules.

I was told about a pack of dogs that continued to come around this house. After further discussion, it was apparent what the problem was. The lady of the house would throw scraps of food out the back door thinking the birds would like them. Instead of the birds getting the first taste, the dogs devoured the food. We attract what we feed. We catch fish according to the bait we use.

People who are negative and pessimistic may not realize the reason they feel familiar with this tone, but actually, they are being fed the comments by demons that in turn feed them; in a crazy sort of way, the two become symbiotic. Matthew 12:43-45 says:

When an unclean spirit goes out of a man, he goes through dry places, seeking rest, and finds none. Then he says, "I will return to my house from which I came." And when he comes, he finds it empty, swept, and put in order. Then he goes and takes with him seven other spirits more wicked than himself, and they enter and dwell there; and the last state of that man is worse than the first. So shall it also be with this wicked generation (NKJV).

Jesus is giving us a clear picture how the devil operates among those who are ignorant of his schemes.

The second lesson from this is to note the house was clean but empty; the emptiness left it open for the return of more demons. The Bible tells us we should be filled with the Spirit. Being filled implies more than initial experience, but a continual refreshing and renewal of the Holy Spirit. Since sweet water and bitter water cannot coexist in the same well, we want to keep a fresh passion for the Lord that is the best demon repellant one could have.

Ezekiel 28:12-17 is a great description of what lucifer was created to be. In short, he was created to be the worship leader in Heaven. His body was created for sound. Every sound and frequency of the sound spectrum was in him. He was like a one-man band to coin a phrase. In him were percussion, wind, and string instruments. He was made for light and sound. Ezekiel 28:14 described him as a covering cherub. Cherubs are angels associated closely with the throne room of God and His presence. Lucifer was called a morning star (Isa. 14:12 NIV). The Son of God was called *"The Bright and Morning Star"* (Rev. 22:16). In these passages of Ezekiel, the prophet describes him as one filled with pride who coveted the worship going to God. The first war in Heaven was over worship. Who will be worshipped? He was thrown down to earth from being filled with light to now being filled with darkness and hatred for the redeemed.

Today, he still uses sound to bring people to himself. He once was created for worship, and now he will do anything to corrupt the worship that belongs to our Lord and Redeemer. He will distract you so you will be too busy to worship. He will use the sound of another voice to bring accusation or offense to interrupt worship. For him, the war over worship continues every day.

In Luke 4:6-7 we read, "*The devil said to Him, (Jesus) 'All this authority I will give you, and their glory; for this has been delivered to me, and I give it to whomever I wish. Therefore if you will worship before me, all this will be yours.' Jesus answers the devil it is written; 'Thou shalt worship the Lord your God, and Him only shall you worship'*" (NKJV). The devil was still trying to get worship from none other than the "*seed that will crush your head*" (Gen. 3:15). The devil knew if he could get Jesus to bow down and relinquish His authority, then he would have full control. The devil even presented the half-truth about giving Jesus authority over the world. Jesus the Son was involved with creation. The devil was a squatter on the earth.

I hope you can see worship is a huge battle with the devil. He understands the power and authority given to worshippers. Just singing songs from a projector screen is what many do, but those who go to the next depth and become immersed by the Spirit to express extravagant love to the lover of our soul, are given access into the throne of grace. Isaiah 35:8-10; describes this position or the redeemed on a highway of Holiness, and no ravenous beast will be allowed there and the redeemed of the Lord will walk there and come to Zion (place of worship) with singing and joy on their heads and joy and gladness shall be their portion and sorrow will have to flee. The life of a person who has a revelation of what it means to be free will experience liberty to worship like never before. The freedom to worship was the very thing the devil wanted to take from us. Slaves have no songs of victory only sorrow and hopelessness. The worship of our Redeemer is liberating and enforces the victory He purchased on the cross.

THE LAST WAR

Revelation 11:1-2 says, *"And then I was given a reed like a measuring rod. And the angel stood, saying, Rise and measure the temple of God, the altar, and those who worship there. But leave out the court which, is outside the temple, and do not measure it, for it has been given to the Gentiles. They will tread the holy city underfoot for forty-two months"* (NKJV).

Worship is viewed here as so important that it is to be measured— the altar and all the worshippers. When God measures something, it is not because He doesn't know the dimensions, but it is for marking those who are worshipping Him. I think it is interesting; the antichrist attempts to mark those who will worship the beast as well. The devil can only counterfeit and copy God. Since he doesn't have the ability to create anything, all he can do is pollute what is sacred to God.

Around special sacred holidays such as Resurrection Day and Christmas, alternate forms of visuals minimize the opportunity to set aside time to truly worship the birth and resurrection of the one who rescued us from destruction. Santa is marketed above the birth of Jesus and the Easter bunny steps in front of the resurrection of our Redeemer.

I hope by now you can see how worship is such a huge part of the power of redemption and that is why the devil will attempt to divert attention from worshipping the one who has crushed his head. We can also understand why he is afraid of the redeemed ones who carry the Spirit of Redemption who also can crush his head. If worship can be measured from God's point of view, then I absolutely want to ensure I don't neglect such a major responsibility to worship without reserve of myself.

Revelation 14:9-10 tells us the last war will again be over worship. The last attempt of the devil and his antichrist to extort worship from the earth will be the final battle. *"Then a third angel followed them, saying with a loud voice, 'If anyone worships the beast and his image, and receives his mark on their foreheads or on his hand, he himself shall also drink of the wine of the wrath of God'"* (NKJV). Worship in its fullness is a sign of submission. The devil knows if he gains worship from the earth, it will be his way of getting ultimate submission. We should know when we truly worship; it is our act of submission to God. For one to just sit back and enjoy the music in worship time is not submission, but only observation. The Kingdom of God does not come by observation, but the kingdom is within you (Luke 17:21). The worship of our King is never meant to be expressed and only observed.

The enemy knows worship is a weapon that moves the Heart of God and dispatches angels. We see this played out in Acts 16:25 when Paul and Silas were put in prison for casting a demon out of a girl whose masters were profiting from the spirit divination. Paul and Silas did not know if they were going to live or be executed because there had been recent executions of believers. Instead of complaining and giving into fear; at midnight, Paul and Silas were praying and singing hymns to God (not to one another), and the prisoners were listening. Suddenly, there was a great earthquake and foundations of the prison *were shaken and immediately all the doors were opened and everyone's chains were loosed.* When true worship was directed to God and not for an earthly audience, everything changed from danger to revival. The jailer and his entire household received salvation. What the enemy meant to silence this apostle and prophet was turned into victory by doing what we are called to do, and that is to worship. No wonder this war in the Heavens is over worship.

Psalm 149:6-9 says, *"Let the high praises of God be in their mouth, and a two-edged sword in their hand, to execute vengeance on the nations and punishment on the peoples to bind their kings with chains and their nobles with fetters of iron to execute on them the judgment written; this is an honor for all His godly ones."*

The weapon of praise coming out of our mouth is a weapon the enemy fears and knows its power because it is partnered with the Heavenly Host, and Jesus is the Captain of this host of angels. Hebrews 4:12 using similar language in describing the Word of God, calls it a two-edged sword. The two-edged sword is translated (*distomos*) meaning two mouths.[1]

Spiritual law says there must be the mouths of two witnesses to establish something as true. (2 Cor. 13:1). The witness of the Word and the enforcement of the Spirit is two mouths, and the witness of our mouth and the mouth of God is also a two-edged sword. The psalmist is connecting praise as two witnesses or mouths strategy of warfare that carries out the written judgment on the enemy. To add to the confirmation is Psalm 48:10 says, *"According to your name, O God, so is Your praise to the ends of the earth"* (NKJV). Simply put, He manifests Himself by the name we praise Him. For instance, if you praise Him as Jehovah-Rapha; "The Lord my God who heals me." The name of God praised reverses the assignment against us and will release the assignment of angels on behalf of us. Psalm 103:20 says, *"Bless the Lord, you His angels, who excel in strength, who do His word, heeding the voice of His word"* (NKJV). The voice of the Lord is half of the two-mouthed sword, and you are the other half resulting in the dispatch of angels with judgment being carried out on the enemy.

In John 4:19-24, Jesus had the conversation with the woman of Samaria at the well. We have already discussed her being an outcast from the community and her poor reputation for having five previous husbands and presently living with a man. She soon realizes by this time Jesus is a prophet. Think for a moment from her position.

She had a prophet standing in front of her; she could ask anything, and He would answer. She could have asked, "Why am I having such rotten luck with men?" or "Why does everybody hate me?" Instead, she asked about worship. Jews say you have to go to Jerusalem to worship while we of Samaria claim another mountain as the place of worship. Jesus blew up both theories by saying; now is the time when the true worshippers will worship in spirit and truth. Jesus coming as the Redeemer everything changed from an outward location of worship to worshipping from the depth of the heart to from the height of some mountain. Verse 23 was the icing when He said, *"The Father is seeking such people to worship Him"* (ESV).

Notice Jesus didn't say God was looking for worship; He was looking for worshippers. God is able to get worship from angels and from the rest of creation. All of creation has a sound even the rocks can cry out (Luke 19:40). The Father is looking for those who have made a choice of their free will to worship with more than lyric and music honoring Him with conduct and behavior.

Our actions reflect what we truly believe more than some sort of philosophy. The way we honor one another has a type of worship connected to it. Honoring the Lord with first fruits by giving and tithing reflects the heart of the worshipper. Jesus said in Matthew 6:21, *"Where your treasure is, there your heart will be also."* The statement is very telling by saying our heart or the inner integrity of who we are, will follow the lead of what we value.

We can document this in a quantitative format. First, look at your schedule or time management device and see where the bulk of your free time outside of mandatory work is used. Then, connect the dots; where do we spend money that is not committed to paying essential bills? Between the two of these—time and money—we can see where our treasure or value really lands. If the heart or inner drive is following these we call treasures; we can see a place of deep motivation. So when the Father says He is seeking worshippers, He is saying He is looking for hearts that are completely His.

Revelation 14:3, gives a description of a song that only the redeemed can sing. Angels can't sing of redemption. We were redeemed and given a free will to worship out of love and thankfulness, not like a CD player which only needs a push a few buttons pushed to get worship. It's not about the style and technique of worship, but the heart of the worshipper. The innate desire in every person is to find their place in creation, to worship God in Spirit and truth.

Truth is not information, but truth is a person called the Spirit of Truth also known as the Holy Spirit. The Holy Spirit knows the mind and will of the Father (1 Cor. 2:10). We need the help of the Holy Spirit to worship the Father in the way that pleases Him. Since worship belongs to God, why not find out what He wants—not what appeals to our taste in music.

When you have a revelation of who God really is, then you worship Him as a speaking spirit and tell Him, "I love You, God. I love You more than anything else. I love You more than all things in this world. I bless Your name more than all other names. Glory unto You, Lord God." Simply, when you worship wholeheartedly, you are connecting Spirit to spirit.

Jesus was communicating intimately with this woman at the well. Her unfulfilled hunger not found in men or natural water will be fulfilled in the person of the Tree of Life, Jesus Christ, who freely gives living water to all who ask.

I am reminded of a conversation I had with a lady after church one morning. She explained how she was not able to fully express herself that morning because they did not sing her song.

"I didn't realize you had written a song."

"No, I haven't written any songs."

I soon got the picture of what she was saying. She was motivated by a certain tempo and style to feel good about herself in worship. I think there are many like her that consider singing as a satisfying activity to us and perhaps still not worship. If our concentration is on the music or style, then our heart maybe following a lesser prompting.

The Holy Spirit inside of us can become a worship leader directing our thoughts and love toward God. Don't get me wrong; I love the corporate times we are being led by a skillful team of musicians and worshippers. I have my favorite genre of songs like all of you; my point is not to let someone do my worship for me as if I was a spectator at a concert being entertained by all the sounds and sights of the room. I have been in African churches with a dirt floor without electricity, and the only musical instrument was a hollowed out log with an animal skin stretched over for a drum, and wow; we experienced deep love and adoration toward our Father in Heaven.

I love certain worship songs that evoke beautiful aspects of my love for the Lord. When we sing about the blood, I'm immediately on my feet. It stirs something covenantal. Allow the Spirit of Truth to guide you into worship. When the Spirit of Truth is present, deep will call out to deep.

WORSHIP THAT AFFECTS THE ATMOSPHERE

A speaking spirit says to something that's dead, *Come alive and come alive and come alive!* Instead of complaining to God how dry and desolate something is, speak to what God intended—abundant life! Psalm 84:5-6 says, *"Blessed is the man whose strength is in You whose heart is set on pilgrimage. As they pass through the Valley of Bacca, they make it a spring; the rain also covers it with pools"* (NKJV). The valley the psalmist mentions is a dry arid region not known for a water supply. This psalm is a picture of one making their pilgrimage to the holy city, and en route there will be this difficult, dry place to pass through. The instruction is when you pass through this in life, change the environment from being a dry place by bringing life into a barren place.

Worship changes the atmosphere and causes water, a sign of life, to spring up and create pools for others to drink from who are following you. The redeemed of the Lord are the only ones who have this gift. Again, let the redeemed of the Lord say so who has been redeemed from the enemy. The song of the redeemed is transformative from death to life just like we were translated out of the kingdom of darkness into the Kingdom of light.

FROM DEATH TO LIFE

A few years ago, I saw what I am describing firsthand. I was asked to minister in a city I had never been in a church I was not familiar with or affiliated with. The meeting opened with prayer, but it was more like a funeral eulogy describing all the sickness and problems of the week and why various ones were not there for the meeting.

When it came time for me to get up, I felt like I weighed five hundred pounds. I was fighting feelings of why I had come to this dead place and how I could quickly end this and get out of there. I tried everything I could from telling jokes to trying to preach. Finally, I heard the Holy Spirit whisper to me; "why don't you sing." I thought now who's telling the jokes; you are kidding me; you have heard me sing, this would only depress everyone more. He continued to press me to change the atmosphere. I began to sing what the Bible calls a "New Song" (Ps. 96:1). This is a song that is spontaneous much like prophecy. I sang about the beauty of the Lord and His love extended to us through His blood. I was shocked and amazed to see people getting to their feet worshipping and lifting a shout unto the Lord.

When I got there, it was a textbook case of the Valley of Bacca; dry and desolate but what I discovered was the wells were buried in years of discouragement and a lack of leadership to lead them through that valley. It began as a death-valley meeting and turned into a downpour. Worship changed the atmosphere like someone changing a thermostat instead of reporting the thermometer. The worship of one redeemed person can bring back to life what God had intended from the beginning.

Philippians 3:3 tells us, *"For we are the circumcision, who worship God in the Spirit, rejoice in Christ Jesus and have no confidence in the flesh"* (NKJV).

Paul was giving a warning in the previous verses concerning those who would take what was part of their covenant and corrupt it. He was referring to himself as part of the circumcision who is identified with the old covenant, but there were those who wanted to use circumcision as an excuse to validate mutilation of the body. The distinction he made was that not only Jews practiced circumcision, but they were worshippers who worship God not because they had been circumcised, but because they were being led by the Spirit. He further admonishes them to rejoice; meaning, be exuberant and expressive in worshipping the Lord and take no confidence in the cutting away of the flesh in circumcision. The picture Paul is making is that it's not the outward keeping of the law, but the internal heartfelt love for Jesus that makes one free.

Colossians 3:16 says, *"Let the word of Christ richly dwell within you, with all wisdom teaching and admonishing one another with psalms and hymns and spiritual songs, singing with thankfulness in your hearts to God."*

And Ephesians 5:19 says, *"Speaking to one another in psalms and hymns and spiritual songs, singing and making melody with your heart to the Lord."*

When a song just bubbles up from within us, it's called a (*těhillah*) spontaneous song or new song of the Lord.[2] Every one of us has a song to sing, and the enemy wants to shut down the song because your song is an anthem of freedom.

BOASTING

When we boast in the Lord, we make Him larger than our enemy. When we boast in the Lord and say He is the Lord our God who heals us, we are making Him bigger than the sickness that has us bound physically. Whatever we talk about the most is what we empower. Whatever you talk about most is what you value and worship.

> But those who wish to boast should boast in this alone: that they truly know me and understand that I am the Lord who demonstrates unfailing love and who brings justice and righteousness to the earth, and that I delight in these things. I, the Lord, have spoken! (Jer. 9:24 NLT).

When we boast in the Lord, we make Him larger than our enemy. When we boast in the Lord and say that He is the Lord our God who heals us, we are making Him bigger than the sickness that has us bound up physically. Whatever we talk about the most is what we empower. Proverbs 23:7 says as one thinks in their heart, so is he. The more we boast in our God, the more we become like Him. Whatever we behold, we will become.

When David was facing Goliath; the giant started the trash talk trying to intimidate David. Goliath was trying to paint a picture in David's mind that the birds of the air would feed on his dead carcass (1 Sam. 17:44-46) David made his boast in the Lord by saying, *"You come to me with a sword, a spear, and a javelin but I come to you in the name of the Lord of hosts, the God of the armies of Israel"* (v. 45). David's attention was upon the power of God to deliver Israel, not on the size of the giant or what he was saying. Singing your boast to the Lord is magnifying His name over the circumstance. The power of the Redeemed carries a song of deliverance. Psalm 32:7 says, *"You are my hiding place; you shall preserve me from trouble; you shall surround me with songs of deliverance"* (NKJV).

Second Corinthians 3:18 tells us: *"But we all, with unveiled face, beholding as in a mirror the glory of the Lord, are being transformed into the same image from glory to glory, just as by the Spirit of the Lord"* (NKJV).

The battle of the mind is one we have to win every day. It is easy to pick up a wrong thought or tone from someone we are working with. That translates into an image or picture. Before we know it, we have an entire feature-length film running through our minds. The enemy attempts to superimpose on our memory banks offenses that keep replaying. We can replace the recordings with new ones.

Start by making your boast on the faithfulness of God and add lots of colorful descriptive words to describe His beauty to us. Read Song of Solomon and pick up the tenderness and intimate bridal language and recite it again and again until you have a fresh new image. Every time the old image and thoughts start previewing in your mind, quickly start replying with your songs of deliverance and be filled with His images of who you are.

You were created with sound and beauty. You are a one-man/woman band. Your vocal chords are stringed instruments you have breath that gives you the wind instruments and your hands clap to make up the percussion section. You are wonderfully and fearfully made (Ps. 139:14). Your sound and your song are distinct to Heaven like a fingerprint identifying you on earth. Proclaim what you are claiming because it is your rights as a redeemed citizen of Heaven.

Lord Jesus, make us aware of the song You have given us to sing. A song never written by anyone on earth. Write it upon our heart so we can sing our own deliverance. Bring us into a greater place of intimacy with You so we can see Your beauty and never doubt our rights as redeemed ones. We belong to You because You purchased us with Your own blood. Let Your word become so deep inside us that it becomes a reservoir of songs to boast in You. Amen!

CHAPTER 5

THE VIOLENT TAKE
IT BY FORCE

IN THIS CHAPTER, we will see what it means to be taking advantage of all the benefits of redemption. John 10:10 is a very familiar verse to many: *"The thief comes only to steal and kill and destroy; I came that they may have life, and have it abundantly."* I discussed in an earlier chapter the three objectives the thief will attempt to use to regain control over a redeemed individual.

Jesus answers the agenda of the thief by coming in the opposite spirit. Where the thief attempts to take freedom from you, Jesus, as the True Shepherd, comes to give life and to give life in abundance or in every part of your life and concern. Jesus used the word life to counter the destruction of the thief. *Zoe* is the Greek word for life meaning strong vitality depicting one who is not weak or anemic.[1] The redemptive work of Jesus doesn't leave us without the ability to resist the devil. He goes beyond giving us life but into abundant life. Abundance in the Greek is *perissos*, meaning beyond expectation to the point of excessive.[2] It also includes life all around you, and in every part of your life. Abundant life is not just a benefit to you, but it affects those around you. The idea of abundance is to have more than what you need but to exceed your need as to fill up the needs around you.

The devil wants you to be need-conscious or self-inspecting. When we take inventory of our needs, we seem always to come up short. Whereas, with abundance, we are looking at the supply of the Redeemer and what He wants to distribute through us.

Before redemption, we were spiritual slaves who only were allowed to have what it took to survive so we could serve another day. Some reading this may see this as describing you now. You may be a redeemed person who has yet to catch a revelation of what Jesus purchased on your behalf. This is why we need to have our minds renewed to match our new status as those who have the right to expect more than enough.

Jesus purchased our freedom to be distributors, not just consumers. You have been born again into the family business where we distribute what has been given to us, and the cycle of inflow will always exceed the outflow if we don't stop giving. When Jesus told the disciples to feed the multitude, they responded by saying they didn't have enough compared to the need (Matt. 14:13-21, Mark 6:30-44, Luke 9:10-17, John 6:1-15). They only had a little bread and a few fish; what is this compared to over five thousand people? Jesus response to them was simply, "it is enough." It is always enough when we look at it from a redemptive opportunity and not a mathematical problem. How we view our position as a redeemed son is the difference between a son and an orphan.

Let's put abundant life into a full and complete definition. I have come to resist the devil through giving you a strong life with vitality beyond what you could have anticipated, and you will not lack in any area of this life. God's redemptive plan was to restore mankind to the place of governing and being afraid of an enemy.

Adam was given dominion in The Garden though the enemy was there as well. Adam had the abundance of life while living in the domain of God's authority. It was only penetrated when he and Eve believed the lie that God was keeping them from something better. When the serpent logically introduced the thought, *"if you eat this you will become like God."* (Gen. 3:5). The appeal was to be closer to God by eating from the forbidden tree, which was disobedience. The thief, in this case, wants to separate them from the seat of dominion wherein lays the abundant life. In essence, the devil was saying go ahead and eat because when you become like God, you will no longer need Him and thus making you independent of Him. An independent spirit always separates us from God and leads to lack. Adam's place of dominion and governing was directly connected to his dependence upon God. The devil had to separate Adam from that seat of authority to take back the governing of the earth.

The redemptive call is for all who have lost their place of abundant life and settled for surviving in an environment where the thief rules and is continually stealing all joy out of life. I have a word for you. Your redemption is near you; simply push back against the tormenting spirit controlling your abundance. Break out of this cycle of control because you were created to be free with an excessive abundance of joy and peace. Let your mind get so filled with God's design for you so you won't be drug back into the domain of darkness again.

As you have been translated out of darkness, you now have the authority of light to destroy darkness. The light shone in the darkness, and the darkness couldn't overcome, comprehend, or out-think it. And also by that authority you're now operating under, the power of redemption gives you the right to believe for supernatural things and a supernatural life!

LIFE CROWDS OUT DEATH

While traveling abroad, I was asked to share a message on the Partnership with the Holy Spirit. Before the meeting started and people were still coming in, a woman came up to me and in a matter-of-fact kind of way introduced herself. She shared her name and said, "I am a meth addict since I was very young." She smiled as she gave the introduction and sat down in the front row. I have never met anyone who has introduced themselves that way without any apparent shame.

When it came time for me to start the message, there she sat directly in front of me. I heard the Holy Spirit, "how long will you wait to set her free?" My first response to the prompting of the Holy Spirit was, "after all the years, why me, why now, surely somebody before now has attempted to free her." I knew I was not going to be able to get into the message on Partnering with the Holy Spirit until I acted in partnership with the Holy Spirit.

I stepped toward her not knowing what I would say or do next in light of my past experience with addicts, which were cumbersome and difficult. I said to her in a loud voice surprising myself, "Who told you that you are a drug addict; quit giving yourself permission to fail, you are a daughter of the Most High God; now stop it." I was not sure how she took it, but at least, I felt better and was able to move on with the message and ministry to the rest of the people in attendance.

A few months later, I received an email from the lady. She told me she went home that evening and did not use any drugs that night and the same for the next several days. In another six months after that, she emailed again testifying how she was completely clean and drug-free. Another email months later revealed she was enrolled in Bible school and was driving again and able to have a relationship with her family again. She had believed a lie for years that her identity was a drug addict and she accepted that as if it were a career choice. When a new redemptive way of thinking entered her thinking, something flipped inside her. The power of addiction was immediately broken, and the thief could not control her thinking anymore.

THE VIOLENT TAKE IT BY FORCE

Matthew 11:12 says, *"From the days of John the Baptist until now the kingdom of heaven suffers violence and violent men take it by force."* Every time I heard someone preach from this text, it was usually used to describe some who had extreme passion or zeal. Some would teach it for the encouragement of being more militant by shouting out. In actuality, it doesn't mean any of that.

The word violent is *biazō* in the Greek. It means to squeeze or crowd out.[3] The idea is not to leave room for anything else. In the previous verse, Jesus was honoring John the Baptist and that there was no one ever been born greater than John. After saying this, He said, *"who is least in the kingdom of heaven is greater than [John the Baptist]"* (Matt. 11:11). At first, it could sound as if John was honored and then it was taken away. Jesus was making a distinction that in the era John lived in, he was the greatest and had great influence.

John preached about the Kingdom, but something was changing. It was changing from an old covenant to the new covenant. Those who enter into the Kingdom have greater power and authority that John who only could preach about the Kingdom. Jesus was explaining that the change between the old and new was causing things to be crowded out or squeezed if you will, and those who enter into this covenant will not have room to bring the old into the new.

The lady who was set free from addiction was experiencing this transformation. She could not enter into the life of abundance with the baggage of a slave. Slaves wore clothes that revealed their life of mediocrity, but garments of abundant life are one of royalty and identify with the family of God. Her drug addiction identified her with darkness all the while she loved God, but she had not experienced the crowding out of the old. Paul the apostle said in Second Corinthians 5:17, *"If anyone is in Christ, he is a new creation; old things have passed away; and behold, all things have become new"* (NKJV).

For things to become new, there must be a crowding out of the old. Bitter water and sweet water cannot come out of the same fountain because one will overtake the other. Jesus did not pay the ultimate sacrifice for us to carry an old self into the new creation. You may feel the conviction of the Holy Spirit as you read this. If you do, then you are feeling the squeezing of the Spirit preparing you for not just life but abundant life.

Matthew 19:23-24 says, *"Assuredly, I say to you that it is hard for a rich man to enter the kingdom of heaven. And again I say to you, it is easier for a camel to go through the eye of a needle than for a rich man to enter the kingdom of God"* (NKJV).

Jesus is using some colorful language depicting those who carry their wealth as their identity and see it as an attachment. They were known for their wealth as their accomplishment, instead of seeing it as a gift of God. The eye of a needle was also an archway that caravans would have to pass under to get into the city. Before they could get their camel to pass through the small archway, they would have to off-load the goods they were bringing into the city.[4] It was a way to make sure no one was carrying contraband into the city. It was perhaps similar to our customs and immigration gates. Jesus was using this analogy to show that those who won't off-load their stuff can't come into the kingdom of God. This narrow passage is similar to what Jesus said in Matthew 7:13, *"Enter by the narrow gate; for wide is the gate and broad is the way that leads to destruction, and there are many who go in by it"* (NKJV).

The violent crowding out is part of God's redemptive grace to bring us into the promise of an abundant life where the thief has not been given a place to attack from. The Bible also says *"Submit yourselves, then to God. Resist the devil, and he will flee from you"* (James 4:7 NIV). The first action must be to submit to God and let Him crowd out all the bitterness and baggage because you can't take it into the new life of freedom.

When I first started pastoring and was still green in leading people, a seasoned pastor spent time with me to help me get past all my inhibitions. He shared something that helped me understand the crowding out process of the Holy Spirit. John told me of how another pastor from a large church on the other side of the city had called him. The pastor said to John, "You have been stealing my sheep."

John kind of chuckled and said, "I don't own any sheep, but I do understand your problem."

The pastor said, "Please explain what my problem is."

John replied, "Well, you have a hole in your fence, and the sheep are crawling through it getting on my side eating the green grass, and they are getting too fat to crawl back through. That is how breakthrough happens."

When someone outgrows the offenses they have had to overcome, the devil can easily attack and break through. The Holy Spirit will show what is causing the setbacks, and when we admit to the baggage, it will fall off, and we can pass through the narrow place to move into the redemptive place of abundance.

Again Jesus, our Redeemer, came to bring us life and life abundantly. In the life He brings to us, spiritual weapons associated with His abundant life empower us while here in this physical life. These weapons are used in exercising authority, not over flesh and blood, but against principalities and powers of darkness (Eph. 6:12). The authority of the abundant life gives us the rights of the redeemed to use. Jesus tells us in John 14:12 we would be able to do greater works because He was going to the Father. To do the things Jesus did, we must have the same life-giving spirit He had while on earth. The Holy Spirit now dwelling in every redeemed person carries life inside you. Dead people can't do life things.

The four weapons against death and destruction are actually four life-carrying aspects of the supernatural realm. Since Jesus came to bring us life, we should look at the four elements or weapons the Bible says has life in them.

1. Life is in the blood.

2. Life is in the seed.

3. Life is in the power of the tongue.

NUMBER I: LIFE IS IN THE BLOOD

The power of the blood is one of my favorite subjects. In Leviticus 17, God mentions the shedding of blood for the first time. The Bible doesn't say explicitly, but the first time that blood was shed was due to Adam and Eve's sin when the animals in The Garden had to be killed so the skins could be used to cover the couple. The principle applies to the One who had to die to cover the sin of humankind forever. Much more than cover it; sin was completely washed away by the sacrifice Jesus made on the cross.

Leviticus 17:11 says: *"For the life of the flesh is in the blood, and I have given it to you on the altar to make atonement for your souls; for it is the blood by reason of the life that makes atonement."* God gave Himself to us upon the altar to make atonement. Atonement doesn't mean to pay a price that's offered; it is the atonement of your soul, for it is the blood that makes atonement for the soul.

If we take apart the word "atonement" and focus on the word "tone," we may think of monotones, microtones, overtones, etc. A tone is a musical or vocal sound with reference to its pitch, quality, and strength— or harmonization. So when God says He has given the blood as atonement, He has harmonized, has once again come into harmony with His created humans.

"When I atone" means I've come into harmony with, I agree with. If I want to buy something that is 20 dollars and I give the clerk 18 dollars, I would not be in agreement. I owe more. When Jesus gave His life and shed His blood, He atoned. All are in agreement, and Heaven is in agreement. Jesus paid the full price for us; Adam's sin will no longer sound out against mankind.

Music is an international language. No matter what language is spoken by the people, middle C is middle C in every country. When you hit middle C, everybody can tune in and knows the tone. Likewise, a blood sound comes up from the earth. Well, there is a tone, atonement, and a harmony that was lost when Adam and Eve disobeyed God. We were out of agreement, against God—*for all have sinned and come short* (Rom. 3:23 KJV). After the Fall of Man, we were short of glory.

And so when He hung on the cross and gave us His life-blood as atonement or an agreement for the payment; His blood made atonement for our souls, the flesh.

Leviticus 17:14 says, *"The life of every creature is in its blood. That is why I have said to the people of Israel, 'You must never eat or drink blood, for the life of any creature is in its blood.' So whoever consumes blood will be cut off from the community"* (NLT). One reason God gave this admonishment was to keep the people from becoming ill; disease was carried through the blood as well. He was giving not only a health law but a spiritual law.

Many generations after Leviticus was written, Jesus said, *"But anyone who eats my flesh and drinks my blood has eternal life, and I will raise that person at the last day"* (John 6:54 NLT). What was He actually saying? His disciples knew what the law said about never eating or drinking blood. Moses wrote down this command from the Lord. Now Jesus says, *"Whoever eats my flesh and drinks my blood remains in me, and I in them"* (John 6:56 NIV). So how could He be the Messiah if He's violating the Levitical law?

But Jesus was talking about the *life* in the blood; He said, *"Unless you eat My life, you won't have My life"* (John 6:53). It's no wonder Jesus is called the bread that came down from above. No wonder the table of showbread was called the Table of Faces, to have an encounter with the Lord.[5] It's no wonder Jesus *"took bread, gave thanks and broke it, and gave it to them, saying, 'This is my body given for you; do this in remembrance of me'"* (Luke 22:19 NIV). He was demonstrating, wanting them—and us—to know His life had value and we could carry the same life through life-blood.

When Jesus was going to Jerusalem, Peter stopped Him and told Him not to proceed because He would be killed. Jesus looked at Peter and said, *"Get behind me, Satan! You are a stumbling block to me; you do not have in mind the concerns of God, but merely human concerns"* (Matt. 16:23 NIV). He was saying that Peter's agenda was for his ministry, but Jesus' agenda was to surrender His sinless blood to redeem all mankind. Peter thought if Jesus went into Jerusalem and was killed, their ministry of traveling around with "the man" preaching and healing people would end. He liked seeing the crowds fed miraculously and all the miracles that happened when Jesus was around. It was pretty cool. But now Jesus was going to ruin everything. Peter was hoping Jesus would kick out the Roman occupation and maybe he would be His right-hand guy. Peter's agenda was very narrowly focused. Jesus' agenda was for eternity. Peter's selfish agenda was for the moment. Jesus' agenda meant giving His life as ransom, atonement, and harmony between Heaven and earth, but Peter at that time couldn't see past his own desires.

FIRST HUMAN BLOOD SHED

Genesis 4 tells the story of Cain and Abel—sons of Adam and Eve. Sin began with the first couple and then entered into the family. The bloodline is corrupt. God accepted Abel's sacrifice, and Cain was jealous. Evidently, the first family understood what God was requiring. Abel presented the Lord with the firstborn of his flock. However, Cain gave God an offering from the fruit of the ground. Cain must have understood what God expected. Otherwise, God would not have rebuked him when he offered what he preferred.

I think it is important to see what was taking place that day. We are told God had regard for Abel's sacrifice, but he did not regard Cain's sacrifice. You would think Cain would have been accepted since he was the firstborn. The issue was not the birth order; it was the sacrifice. The rebellious heart of Cain was refusing to ask his brother for a lamb to give a blood sacrifice. Most scholars believe God would send fire upon the altar of any sacrifice He received. Can you imagine two altars both had their sacrifices ready, waiting for God's approval when suddenly fire came down and consumed Abel's sacrifice and Cain's was just sitting there without regard? The word regard means to receive attention. Abel received the attention from God and Cain was ignored.

"The Lord accepted Abel and his gift, but he did not accept Cain and his gift. This made Cain very angry, and he looked dejected" (Gen. 4:4-5 NLT). Do you want to catch God's attention? Give Him what He asks for. "'Why are you so angry?' the Lord asked Cain. 'Why do you look so dejected? You will be accepted if you do what is right. But if you refuse to do what is right, then watch out! Sin is crouching at the door, eager to control you. But you must subdue it and be its master'" (Gen. 4:6-7 NLT).

Sin lies at the door, the entranceway into your life, and its desire is to control, manipulate, and enslave you—but you should rule over it. God gave Cain the power to rule over sin, just as He has given you the power to rule over it, but Cain chose not to subdue it. Cain took the option of a bloodless sacrifice, thus rejecting the life God He wanted to cover him with. Cain's independence was closely similar to the serpent with an independent spirit. Because he chose to live without the life of God, murder entered his heart. *"One day Cain suggested to his brother, 'Let's go out into the fields.' And while they were in the field, Cain attacked his brother, Abel, and killed him"* (Gen. 4:8 NLT).

After Cain killed his brother, the Lord asked Cain, *"'Where is your brother? Where is Abel?' 'I don't know,' Cain responded. 'Am I my brother's guardian?' But the Lord said, 'What have you done? Listen! Your brother's blood cries out to me from the ground! Now you are cursed and banished from the ground, which has swallowed your brother's blood'"* (Gen. 4:9-11 NLT).

THE SOUND OF BLOOD

Blood has a sound that God can hear: *"Your brother's blood cries out to me...."* Likewise, Jesus tells us that if we don't praise and worship the Lord, the very rocks will cry out (Luke 19:40). Everything God created absorbs sound. All molecular matter absorbs sound. God created the earth by speaking into the substance, and it came together to form His imagination/image. That is why it still carries His sound. Have you ever heard someone say, "If these walls could talk?" Walls actually do absorb sound. Let's take this fact a step further. If your home is full of screaming and yelling, or if it is full of laughter and gentle conversation, a tone is set in the household.

All of creation carries the voice of God. The Bible says that creation shouts His worth. But rocks aren't redeemed; they're just created.

Angels are created; they're not redeemed. Things are created—only humans carry the potential of being redeemed. And God says He would rather hear from us than creation itself. The life is in the blood. We carry a sound inside us. What sound we're giving off is the sound or the relationship we have with Jesus Christ. Jesus was teaching His disciples how to serve as they travel from city to city, in Matthew 10:13, *"If the household is worthy, let your peace come upon it. But if it is not worthy, let it return to you"* (NKJV).

A home has an environment about it that is created by those who are blessing or cursing in the home. Jesus is teaching that if a home has a sound in tune with you, bless that home by releasing your peace over the home. In the same way, the blood cries out over us saying: Life. Before Jesus, blood was spilled, beginning the transition from the old covenant to the new covenant; blood was seen as a prophetic sign of a new day coming.

In Exodus 12 is the account of the Hebrews being brought out of Egyptian slavery. They had been slaves for 430 years; generations of Hebrews knew nothing more than slavery. God sent Moses to lead them out of the captivity. God gave Moses the authority to release judgment on Egypt until they would release the captive Hebrews. God was going to send a death angel that would strike all firstborn. The sign of separation between the death angel and the Hebrews would be blood on the doorposts of their house. Verse 13 tells us, *"The blood shall be a sign for you on the house where you are. And when I see the blood, I will pass over you; and the plague shall not be on you to destroy you when I strike the land of Egypt"* (NKJV). The blood of a lamb they chose was placed on the doorpost showing the house was worthy of life. All who were in the house had life, and those outside received judgment. The blood cried out "Passover," and so the blood became a protection for those who obeyed.

Cain had known the same instruction as Abel but chose death over life. We are covered today by the sound of the blood of the Lamb and allow His peace to come upon our home. Proverbs 18:21 says the power of life and death is in the tongue. The tongue produces sounds into words. Those words or sounds either cause life or they cause death. They are either full of healing or poison.

When I was a kid, we used to hunt rabbits, coyotes, and other varmints. One time I heard a rabbit crying out a shrill, morbid sound. All of a sudden I saw eyes popping open in the dark going after the sound. The rabbit's distress sound attracted predators to him. The Bible says, *"The devil, prowls around as a roaring lion, seeking someone to devour"* (1 Pet. 5:8). Is it possible we give off a sound that draws the hordes of hell? Do we give off a sound that harmonizes with the devil?

Philippians 1:28 says fear is a sign to your enemy of perdition. Perdition means to fall away or to lean away from your goal. If we are falling backward, we have no strength. Those who know anything about boxing know you can't throw a punch at your opponent with any force if you're on your heels. That is why you see them always on their toes bouncing and weaving. You can tell when one of them is losing strength because they begin to be flat-footed and later they are leaning backward. The devil wants to bring some sort of punch through an offense to put you on your heels, so you are losing life and strength.

Complaining and cursing will always be a sound the demons are attracted to. The power of the blood of Jesus has a sound, and the devil has a sound as well. The devil is afraid of the sound of the blood of the Lamb because there is a life-giving sound in the blood. When a husband and wife sit around the table struggling with paying bills, if they are not careful, they will give off a sound like a wounded rabbit just ready for the taking. They say things like, *nothing good ever happens to us. We are never going to get ahead.* The next step is to blame one another for the stress they are under. The devil's food cake comes out, and the demons start feasting and even helping you to think of deadly words to say to each other.

I was asked to speak at a men's retreat in St. Louis, and I was sharing the importance of sound and spiritual connection it has in our lives. I shared how lucifer was created by God for light and sound. When cast out of Heaven, he still tries to control the sound. We all have a sound or song.

There was an experiment done with a mouse that had cancer. The DNA of the sick mouse was connected to a synthesizer, and the cells of the mouse made a mournful sound. The same was done with a healthy mouse, and the sound was a lively sound like a rhythmic waltz.[6] I made a comment at the retreat that our homes are a reflection of either cursing or blessing depending on the sound it absorbs. I even shared the first recorder was in the Bible. Joshua 24:27 says, *"Behold this stone shall be a witness to us, for it has heard all the words of the Lord which He spoke to us. It shall therefore be a witness to you, let you deny your God"* (NKJV). Joshua actually used a stone to record what was said. I know for some that is a stretch but remember Jesus said the rocks would cry out and science concludes that all matter absorbs sounds.

The next Sunday morning, I was to speak at the church that was hosting the retreat. I was walking across the parking lot when one man I recognized from the retreat motioned me to come over to him. He told me that he wasn't quite sure at first if he believed what I had shared on sound. He and his wife were raising their grandson for the last four years, and it had caused division in their home. They were divided over the strategy of raising the grandson.

When he returned home from the retreat, his wife and grandson were out running errands. He remembered what had been said about the house absorbing the sounds and it had certainly not been sounds of blessing. He decided to give it a try; after all, what would it hurt. He went through the house as instructed and repented of all the vile things spoken between him and his wife. He then sat down in his recliner to relax and dozed off. He said, "I would not have believed, had I not been there to witness it myself." When his wife and grandson returned, the normal would have been for the grandson to run all over the house scattering toys and bouncing off the walls and his wife ignoring him. But the opposite happened. The little boy crawled up in his lap and said, "I love you, Paw Paw," and was still enough for him to snuggle up. And then he said, "My wife came over and kissed me on the forehead." He said, "It was as if someone had changed the thermostat of the whole house." The environment was now worthy of peace. There can come a new sound, and it was ministering to all in the house. He realized with all his complaining and feeling like the victim in the house, he was giving off a sound that was attracting a spirit of division.

Psalm 89:15 says, "How blessed are the people who know the joyful sound! O Lord, they walk in the light of Your countenance."

First Corinthians 14:8 tells us, "If the trumpet makes an uncertain sound, who will prepare for battle" (NKJV).

If we are giving off the wrong sound through arguing and divisive behavior, then it would not be unusual to find demonic spirits feeding off the environment we are setting.

If the devil can get you to change your tune, change your sound to one of doom and gloom, then he's succeeded in changing your focus from God to yourself and your current problem. When you sound more like despair than delight, you are losing the battle.

When the blood of Jesus hit the ground while He was hanging on the Cross, *"the earth shook and the rocks were split"* (Matt. 27:51). BOOM! The power of His blood reverberated throughout creation. All of creation that God spoke into existence recognized Jesus' blood, the same spirit that was there in the beginning that overcame darkness. When the last drop of life from Jesus' body fell, creation shook and trembled because the Greater One's power was unleashed in humility—the first step toward His resurrection and our redemption.

The Bible says the earth shook so much that the tombs of some ancient saints were opened. They didn't emerge until after the resurrection, but they were opened (Matt. 27:52-53). Jesus had to take His blood into the Holy of Holies; the Holy of Holies not made by human hands as the one with Moses. The original one is in Heaven according to Hebrews 9:24. When Jesus placed His sinless blood on the mercy seat in Heaven; everything the enemy had power over had been broken, there must have been sounds of glory resonating in all of Heaven.

And Jesus cried out again with a loud voice, and yielded up His spirit. And behold, the veil of the temple was torn in two from top to bottom; and the earth shook and the rocks were split. The tombs were opened, and many bodies of the saints who had fallen asleep were raised; and coming out of the tombs after His resurrection they entered the holy city and appeared to many. Now the centurion, and those who were with him keeping guard over

Jesus, when they saw the earthquake and the things that were happening, became very frightened and said, "Truly this was the Son of God!" (Matthew 27:50-54).

When I was growing up, if I told my mother I wasn't feeling very good and didn't want to go to school, she would call me over to her. First, she would spit on her finger and then wipe it on my forehead (Most people use oil, but she used what she had). Then she would slap her hands down on my shoulders and say, "I speak the blood of Jesus over your body, and no unclean thing shall come here!" Then she would look me in the eyes and say, "You're fine, go to school." I could never get out of going to school. She didn't just believe in the power of the blood for salvation but used the authority of the blood of Jesus to rebuke sickness and any other obstinate attitude she deemed as off limits in her home.

In the name of the Lord Jesus Christ; I ask for violent crowding out of unbelief and doubt for all who read this book. I declare the blood of Jesus as the source of all our rights to reclaim our heritage in the Kingdom of God. I call for all the prodigals to be found and recovered to the place of their calling. I bind any hindrance to the fulfillment of the assignments of my friends, and all will come to the full potential of the seed of Christ. May the Lord bless you with fresh insight to see through His eyes so you would know the hope of His calling. Amen!

CHAPTER 6

LIFE IS IN THE SEED

WE HAVE LEARNED in the previous chapters how Jesus came in the opposite spirit to confront the thief that kills, steals, and destroys. Because He brought life, we should look further at the weapons He gave us that carry life. We began with the Life that is in the blood and the second one is the life that is in the seed.

NUMBER 2: LIFE IS IN THE SEED

Inside each seed is the DNA potential. Wrapped in that tiny seed is a greater potential than appears at first glance. The seed always produces far more than itself. It surpasses the natural to become more than anyone can anticipate.

The devil knows that seed will continue to reproduce exponentially when it is sown. He knows the only way to stop the fruit is to kill the seed that carries the future to destroy him. Genesis 3:15 first mentions the seed as being a weapon. *"I will put enmity between you and the woman, and between your seed and her Seed; He shall bruise your head, and you shall bruise His heel"* (NKJV). This statement is prophetic coming from God to the serpent, the devil. The promise is for there to be a seed from the woman that would bruise the devil's head. The Hebrew word for bruise (*shuwph*) is to overwhelm or break.[1] The seed coming from the woman that could do that is the seed that came from God the Father through Mary. The seed came from the heavenly realm, not from an earthly father.

Every seed carries in itself the same DNA as the original. Every born again redeemed person carries the same DNA as the original seed from God. The seed that bruised the head of the serpent two thousand years ago continues to bruise his today.

For instance, the corn seed when sown will produce a stalk that has multiple ears of corn. Each kernel of corn in that stalk carries the same DNA as the seed that was buried and died to produce the stalk. Each time one kernel of corn is planted and dies, it will produce more than itself.

In John 12:24, Jesus referred to Himself as a seed and said, *"Unless a grain of wheat falls into the earth and dies, it remains alone; but if it dies, it bears much fruit."* Some people thought He was talking about farming. Those who could hear Him as the seed level knew He was speaking prophetically.

The seed that came to bruise the head of the serpent had to be sown. If not sown, it stays alone. Alone in the Greek is the word *monos*, meaning lacking the ability to reproduce.[2] Those who want the increase of God but won't sow their lives into the Kingdom of God, become monos without the ability to be fertile and reproduce.

Peter especially didn't want Jesus to be talking about dying. In Matthew 16:23, Peter tries to talk Jesus out of going into Jerusalem because of the danger of being killed. Jesus rebukes Peter saying, to him *"Get behind Me, Satan! You are an offense to Me, for you are not mindful of the things of God, but the things of men"* (NKJV) Those were strong words for his friend. Jesus knew there was more behind that than just Peter.

Peter perhaps had his own agenda not wanting Jesus to die. Peter, like some of us if we were in that position, wondered what would happen to him if Jesus died. The disciples became really dependent upon Jesus. When they needed tax money, they just went fishing, and there was the tax money in the fish, and now people knew them as one of his close friends. It became trendy to hang out with Jesus at least for a while. Maybe at that time, they saw Jesus as a sort of goose that laid the golden egg. Jesus also recognized the serpent was once again behind the scenes working through Peter thinking he could kill the seed.

John 16:7 says, *"Nevertheless I tell you the truth. It is to your advantage that I go away; for if I do not go away, the Helper will not come to you; but if I depart, I will send Him to you"* (NKJV). Jesus again is shedding light on reproducing this seed into us. If He stays, the seed cannot be scattered because it resides in only Him, but if He returns to His Father, the seed will be multiplied through all that will allow the seed to be implanted. In verse 14, Jesus says, *"He will glorify Me, for He will take of what is Mine and declare it to you"* (NKJV). Jesus told them they would be able to do greater things if He leaves. The greater things are going to surpass the time Jesus was on earth, and it will be multiplied by all those who carry His seed.

Remember, it is the thief who comes to steal, kill, and destroy the seed (John 10:10). The devil is not aware of the plan because the seed he thinks he kills will put an end to the threat of a redeemer. The seed Jesus sowed is now reproducing His DNA in other seed.

The Egyptian pharaoh wanted to kill all the male Hebrew children so that their seed could not grow up and overthrow him. In Matthew 2, Herod ordered the death of male children two years and younger to kill the seed of one whom could overcome him. The thief looks for potential leaders who carry the seed that can bruise his head; to steal purpose and vision to sidetrack them from the purpose of bruising his head.

First John 3:8 tells us the mission of Jesus which should be ours too, *"For this purpose the Son of God was manifested, that He might destroy the works of the devil"* (NKJV). The Holy Spirit will direct us on the strategy to use to destroy the works of the devil. That strategy may entail a particular way to pray to bring down demonic structures. Some will hear strategies of worship that will overwhelm the spirit of darkness in a region. In any case, you carry the seed to use that will multiply and reproduce in others.

THE PRINCIPLE OF SEEDTIME

In Genesis 1:11 we read, *"God said, 'Let the earth bring forth grass, the herb that yields seed, and the fruit tree that yields fruit according to its kind, whose seed is in itself, on the earth'; and it was so."* The creation began with God speaking it into existence so it would continue recreating itself. Seed is a great picture of God's design being activated every day and at seasonal times.

Genesis 8:22 tells us, *"While the earth remains, seedtime and harvest, cold and heat, winter and summer, and day and night shall not cease"* (NKJV). God announces a promise backed up by the covenant sign of the rainbow (Gen. 9:13) that there will always (Gen. 8:22) be seed and harvest. Seeds are an important theme running through the Bible and are a prophetic picture of how creation works and multiplies.

In John 1:1-3, we learn the Word was at the beginning of creation, the Word is God, and all things were made through Him and nothing created was created without the Word. Then in verse 14, we see *"The Word became flesh and we beheld His glory..."* (NKJV). The seed that was in the beginning was also the Word. The word is also seen as seed. Anything created had to have the Word spoken.

When you hear someone say, "The Lord spoke to me" they are not usually talking about an audible voice they hear with their natural hearing senses of the ear. Hearing the voice of the Lord is hearing His word. The word is Jesus speaking to us. Though I won't discount the possibility of an audible voice, most hear Him through His word. Just as in the Genesis account of creation, God spoke into the darkness and the darkness could not push back, and light prevailed. His Word spoken is His voice coming through His Word. His Word dwelled among us, and we were able to behold His Glory.

We can see God's Word had a voice, and His voice today through the Logos or written Word of God has a voice. When the said voice is implanted inside of us and we speak, it becomes a saying or Rhema word. All true revelations that come from God are His voice. Hearing His voice is not difficult when we connect His voice to His Word. His Word is the absolute inerrant word that has a voice. The Holy Spirit is the Spirit of truth. When the Holy Spirit highlights His word, that voice becomes a revelation.

Hebrews 1:3 says, *"Who being the brightness of His glory and the express image of His person, and upholding all things by the word of His power, when He had by Himself purged our sins, sat down at the right hand of the Majesty on High"* (NKJV). His spoken word upholds or rules to the point of enforcing the power of His Word at creation. If we see the depth of His Word now, then we could also feel confident, He is holding us up through enforcing His spoken word. When we pray the Word, we are speaking or praying with creative authority.

Romans 10:17 says, *"So then faith comes by hearing, and hearing by the word of God"* (NKJV). Simply put faith is moving toward what you believe. If what you have heard has not moved or stirred you, then it probably was not heard with faith. The extent of the word is the extent of faith.

There is a difference between listening to something and hearing. Hearing implies self-application to what was heard. For instance, if I am listening to someone talking about their schedule and the many duties they have to do; I am probably just listening with no personal involvement. If they happen to say, "Kerry will be accompanying me at this time" then, all of a sudden, I cease listening, and now I am hearing. Faith comes not by listening but through hearing a personal voice speaking to your heart through His Word that has personal application.

Jesus said in John 10:27, *"My sheep hear My voice"* (NKJV). The way we get to know His voice is through knowing His word. I often joke about my mother; though she has gone to her reward many years ago, I know what she would have said about most things—that is why I can say she is still the voice in my head. That is not a literal voice, but her words of encouragement still speak to me today. The words of Jesus still speak to me every day, and we were created to need that interaction. Jesus quoted from Deuteronomy 8:3 when confronting the devil in the wilderness, *"Man shall not live by bread alone; but man lives by every word that proceeds from the mouth of the Lord"* (NKJV). We were created to have an abundant life when we live from the word spoken from the mouth of God. Again, the Word of God is the voice of God to us.

PRINCIPLE OF CREATION

There is a principle of creation seen through the Bible. For something to be created, it first must be decided as to the substance it will be created from. For instance, man was created physical from the dust of the earth. Part of us relates to the natural earthy origins. We were also created with a spirit. Our spirit came from the substance of God Himself. He breathed into man eternal substance of His own spiritual DNA.

The principle of sustaining creation is also important. Whatever something is created from, it must also be nourished from the same substance. Since we were physical, created from the ground, then we are healthier when we eat plants that come from the ground. The principle is also true with our spirit; the substance that can only come from God—which satisfies the hunger in our spirit—must also nourish us.

God created us to need to be nourished by the word that comes from His mouth. Like bread is to the body, so is the Living Bread, Jesus, to our spirit. When we neglect to feed on His Word, we get weak and susceptible to the temptations that appeal to the flesh. Jesus made this clear after His encounter with the woman at the well in John 4:32 and 34. His disciples returned with the food for the group, and Jesus told them He had meat they were not aware of, which was to do the will of the Father. There is such satisfaction to live by the voice of God speaking through His word and then acting upon it. The Gifts of the Holy Spirit is given to us for the release of the word through us to others. Allowing the Holy Spirit the freedom to minster through us is wonderful and fulfilling.

Romans 12:6 says, *"Having then gifts differing according to the grace that is given to us, let us use them: if prophecy, let us prophesy in proportion to our faith"* (NKJV).

Since faith comes by hearing the Word and we prophesy to the depth or level of faith, then we must recognize that prophecy is closely tied to hearing the Word as well. A little word brings about little faith, and little faith results in little prophecy. Revelation 19:10 adds to this point, *"For the testimony of Jesus is the spirit of prophecy."* Since we have shown that prophecy comes through faith, and faith through hearing; look at the testimony of Jesus which also stems from the voice of the word.

In a court of law if you gave a second-hand account of a crime based on what someone told you that would be deemed hearsay and not an admissible testimony. When one has a firsthand encounter with the voice of the word, we can deem this a true testimony or spirit of prophecy. In the mouth of two witnesses, let every word be established. The witness of the Word and the witness of the Spirit establishes the completion of something. The witness of the Holy Spirit will always draw upon the voice of the word.

THEY HEARD THE VOICE WALKING

Genesis 3:8 tells us, *"They heard the sound of the Lord God walking in the garden in the cool of the day, and Adam and his wife hid themselves from the presence of the Lord God among the trees of the garden"* (NKJV).

There are a few observations from scholars as to the voice of the Lord walking. In any case, there was something heard and perhaps something seen. Using the descriptive term *"the cool of the day"* could suggest a breeze or wind accompanying the sound of His voice. Perhaps it was similar in Acts 2 when the Holy Spirit came rushing into the upper room, or in Job 38:1 where God spoke to Job out of the whirlwind. The main takeaway from our point is they hid from the presence of the Lord. They were accustomed to the nourishing sound of God's presence before their disobedience.

The voice of the Lord even today moves through His Word, and when we are embracing this experience, we are being built up in our spirit to the point we can prophesy with confidence and faith to see the authority reach its creative purpose. The devil will give us plenty of logical excuses to hide ourselves week after week from exposure to God's voice coming through His Word. The devil wasn't showing up while God's voice was walking in The Garden. The devil waits till we are gazing at something God has forbidden and that is when the serpent begins interjecting another voice into our garden or family.

Man lives well when he lives by the Word of God, and he doesn't do so well when he is on a starvation diet in his spirit. Jesus taught us to pray by asking the Father for daily bread. Some view this as asking God for personal sustenance, but I think it also goes beyond the natural to the cry of our heart. What Adam lost in the Garden of Eden; Jesus, our Redeemer, wants to restore the voice of God walking again in our garden. When we pray, we can ask for the bread that proceeds from the mouth of God which enables us to not just live but to live with abundance—the abundance of the word, joy, and of life, whereby we might have more than enough to give to others.

In Luke 8:11, Jesus plainly teaches in this parable that the seed is the Word of God. The majority of the people hearing this parable were an agronomist type people who understood planting seeds. He clearly states the seed in this story is the said Word of God. We can also conclude the seed is God's voice speaking to us. The parable has two main components that connect the four different scenarios of the seed being planted. The two connecting thoughts are the condition of the soil and the extent of one hearing the voice or the Word of God. Let's take a close look at each of the three conditions to being fruitful.

1. Verse 12. The seed sown by the wayside are those who hear; but before the word can be activated in them the devil comes and takes away the word out of their hearts. The hearing is really the condition of the ground. How we hear is the type of ground we are. In each case, the hearing is connected to the preparation of the soil. The seed is good, and the sower is good; only the ground and the hearing which receive the word makes the difference.

There is a difference between hearing and listening. The word hearing is similar to the concept of encountering. Let me give an example of the two.

It was my first time to be the conference speaker in Cuernavaca, Mexico. The church was large, and the building was packed with some standing outside listening through the doors. My plane had arrived late, so when I got there, I was taken through the crowd to a front row seat. The service was ready to start. There was a quiet buzz of expectancy around the auditorium. I noticed in front of me was a stack of audio speakers taller than me. I was listening quietly to those visiting with one another; then suddenly, the meeting started with a full band. The sound that came out of the mammoth speakers went right through me. I ceased listening with my natural ears and began to encounter. My shirt was vibrating from the base frequencies. I was experiencing it more than processing it as a listening ear.

Hearing was meant to be the encountering of the voice of God whether through someone speaking or by reading the Word of God, but it is much more than listening. If we only listen, the seed can be stolen. When we encounter, the seed becomes implanted.

2. Verse 13. The seed sown among the rocks they hear with a sense of joy but have no depth of root. For a while, it seems to be received but has no root system because it could not withstand times of testing.

3. Verse 14. The seed sown among thorns are those who after they have heard go and are choked by the cares of life. The cares of life here is a very telling word. In the Greek, it is the word *merizō* meaning a divided mind or double-minded.[3] There is not a single purpose that causes passion of the heart to fix on one target. It is more than not having enough time in a schedule. It is more about priority or seeking first the Kingdom of God. They are seeking many things and end up with a divided heart and no energy left to give to the lover of your soul. Matthew 6:21 tells us that where our heart is that is where our treasure will be.

The thorns brought a divided mind to the point they are not sure any more what the real treasure is. It implies the riches, and the temporary part of life became dominant, and the eternal part of life took a back seat. Hearing the voice of God was mixed in with a lot of other voices or seeds. Remember, the thorns came from seeds as well.

Many voices are in the world, and they are all clamoring for our attention. The one we hear the most and give the most attention to is the voice we will fellowship with and will reproduce its seed. We become what we behold. Hearing is not a one-time event, but the concept is after having heard, you will continue hearing.

3. Verse 15. The seed that was sown on the good ground heard the word a good heart and kept the seed and bears fruit with patience. Redemption is to be more than delivering us from an evil master but restoring us to a loving God. For that love to continue growing, it will take the restoring of our ability to hear with clarity and courage to react to the seed beyond a level of only believing.

Faith comes by hearing and hearing the word. This parable is about not only hearing but also about how we hear and what we hear. We are to protect our hearing. If our hearing is loaded up with daily garbage and doom from the news, then we have been seeded with a mixture of skepticism and fear. Proverbs 4:23 says, *"Watch over your heart with all diligence, for from it flow the springs of life."*

Since we prophesy from faith, and faith comes by hearing, and our hearing comes from a pure heart, then we can conclude that a guarded heart will produce a more pure prophetic word. The condition of the soil or heart is the only thing that can limit the potential of the seed. Isaiah 55:11 tells us the Word of the Lord *"shall not return to Me void, but it shall accomplish what I please"* (NKJV). A sent word from God will say things to your heart that will cause changes as nothing else will. The only thing we need is to hear with the same purpose it was sent.

The enemy wants to steal, kill, and destroy—especially the seeds God has planted for generations to come. For when you reap the harvest of your sown seeds, you enlarge God's Kingdom. You are the gatekeeper of the seeds as part of your legacy. The thief comes to destroy relationships between fathers and sons. The devil will abort the seed that God said over you if he can.

Guard the seed and protect the harvest in your family by keeping alive the words of God spoken over you and your family. To rehearse means to re-hear. Heart meant to hear it with your spirit. Don't despise the times you retell the stories of the miracles you have witnessed and the promises spoken over you because they will be passed on as the family jewels. Malachi 4:6 gives a strong rebuke by saying, *"He will turn the hearts of the fathers to the children, and the hearts of the children to their fathers, lest I come and strike the earth with a curse"* (NKJV). One reason for the rebuke was because the fathers stopped recounting the stories of the miracles of their deliverance from Egypt. Many generations had passed, and the testimonies about the Passover lamb and God drowning their captors in the Red Sea had faded from the storytelling around the table with the family. Keeping alive the promises of your family is a highly valuable seed to be passed on and lived out, thereby bringing blessing to the family.

Isaiah 54:13 and 17 says your children shall be taught of the Lord and great peace shall be upon them; no weapon formed against them shall prosper and any voice raised in judgment against them shall be found to be false, for this is the heritage or the inheritance of the children of God. Your two-edged sword pierces the darkness and lays an ax to the root of the thing; now you are in agreement with God, and the seed has life in it and will not come back to you empty-handed.

Lord Jesus, help us to be more aware of Your voice speaking to us. We ask for greater sensitivity to Your word. We come today with an open heart ready to receive the implanted seed. I confess my sins today and ask You to remove the thorns from my life that has caused me to have a divided mind. Fill me with the Holy Spirit so I might be led into all the truth You have given to me. Thank You for the power of Your redemption that brings me closer to my destiny. Amen!

CHAPTER 7

THE POWER OF THE TONGUE

The tongue can bring death or life; those who love to talk will reap the consequences.—Proverbs 18:21 NLT

PROVERBS TELLS US there is life and death in what people say. God spoke creation into existence. We, too, speak things into existence. How we speak to one another causes either life or death. As discussed briefly in Chapter 3, we will be judged for every idle word we speak.

NUMBER 3: LIFE IS IN THE POWER OF THE TONGUE

God gave us His Word, the Bible, and He also speaks life through us when we avail our hearts, minds, and tongues to the Holy Spirit. An idle word doesn't just mean a "flippant saying" but it comes from the Greek word *argos* meaning a word that doesn't produce fruit.[1] In essence, an idle word is something unproductive—better still, it does not produce the Fruit of the Spirit. A conversation that has love, joy, peace, longsuffering, gentleness, etc. laced in is a fruit-bearing dialogue.

CURSING AND IDLE WORDS

To curse means to place someone or something in a lower position than God intended. A so-called put-down is a curse. Though it may not seem like something you would call witchcraft, it certainly fits the meaning of cursing.

In Mark Chapter 11 is the account of Jesus cursing the fig tree. The teaching moment with His disciples was a poignant one. They saw on their return walk that the tree had quickly died. Jesus follows up with explaining in verse 23: *"Whoever says to this mountain, 'Be removed and be cast into the sea,' and does not doubt in his heart, but believes that those things he says will be done, he will have whatever he says"* (NKJV).

There are two points to our study here. The first is that we can kill things with our tongue. The power of life and death are present with us at all times. Killing someone with words can kill their passion and dreams for the future.

The second is that speaking to the mountain to be removed is based on not only speaking to the mountain but also believing what you are saying. Many of us are guilty of saying one thing but not really believing what we said. This truth is controversial to some because of people abusing this to get stuff for themselves. They are saying words that are not coupled with believing what one is saying.

To really believe in your heart takes the quickening or the assurance of the Holy Spirit. So, if the Holy Spirit is not prompting what you are saying, then it is idle words. Since faith comes by hearing the word (Rom. 10:17), then it takes the Holy Spirit to bring to life the saying as a

Rhema word to our spirit; otherwise, it's just hollow religious-sounding people with self-induced desires.

In verse 25, Jesus connects forgiveness to this cursing of the fig tree. He said, *"Whenever you stand praying, if you have anything against anyone, forgive him, that your Father in heaven may also forgive you"* (NKJV). Here is a precondition to being effective in speaking the desires of your heart. If there is anything you held against anyone; meaning a point of resistance, forgive them so that you are also forgiven, and thus nothing is resistant to you seeing the desired results.

We probably all have known those who say clichés that sound full, but without the fullness of the Holy Spirit conceiving them in their heart. One can travail and attempt to birth something only to find they had no seed to bring about fruit. In Second Corinthians 3:6 we read, *"Who also made us sufficient as ministers of the new covenant, not of the letter but of the Spirit; for the letter kills, but the Spirit gives life"* (NKJV). The power of life and death is in the tongue or speaking, but the Spirit must be the partner in us speaking the word for it to bring life. Just randomly speaking something we have always used as default quotations may not bring any transformation. However, when the Holy Spirit is prompting us to speak with His leadership, the results become miraculous. Perhaps you are one who has witnessed the abuse or one-sided teaching of the power of the tongue; then I hope this will help you to see the problem was not having the partnership with the Holy Spirit to bring about the expected results. Relying on and waiting for the quickening of the Holy Spirit takes the pressure off you and places the demand upon the Word and the Spirit which are the dynamic duo.

In Second Corinthians 4:13 says, *"Since we have the same spirit of faith, according to what is written, 'I believed and therefore I spoke' we also believe and therefore speak"* (NKJV). Notice the importance of having the same spirit of faith working in Jesus while He was on the earth; we too can speak when we believe what we are saying is of the Spirit. Learning to speak the word is not the main need we need to learn. It is the synchronizing our tongue with the Spirit of Truth. It was the Holy Spirit that was also present at creation. When God spoke, the Holy Spirit brooded or inseminated over the face of the waters. Today, when we speak under the direction of the Holy Spirit, He will move in response to the Word we speak.

There should also be some caution amplified here. The same instrument that carries life as a God-given tool can also be used as an instrument of destruction whereby the devil pounces upon and gives agreement and proceeds to make a doorway. Proverbs 26:2 tells us, *"Like a flitting sparrow, like a flying swallow, so a curse without cause shall not alight"* (NKJV). The illustration of these two types of birds is crucial to understanding how cursing can attach to us, and how to prevent being party to cursing. Here is the concept. A bird flies from one nest to another. When it leaves a nest, it looks for another landing spot. The curse is like a bird looking for a place to land. A curse can't come without a cause or another nest.

When someone is cursing a spouse, child, or perhaps a boss, they are building a landing strip on the one doing the cursing. Again, a curse is saying or declaring someone is in a lower position than what God intended or created them to be. Calling someone a name to put him in a lower, demeaning place is a curse no matter the motivation. If you delight in putting others down, you will not be surprised when you find blocked access to your prayers being answered, and also you will find cursing coming your way because you built a landing strip that a Boeing 747 could land on and unload its cargo.

In Matthew15:11, Jesus said, it's *"Not what goes into the mouth defiles a man; but what comes out of the mouth, this defiles a man"* (NKJV). What comes out of the mouth is sown and affects everyone we are connected with, and it cannot be retrieved. One who is cautious with his words and the effects is a wise person. The old saying "I have a notion to give that person a piece of my mind," reveals a disregard as to the consequences of our words but only to vent our feelings. Feelings can change, but when those feelings spill over into the hearts and minds of others, then those feelings are no longer temporary or internalized, but now they become sown and will reproduce in the memories of others.

James 3:2-10 describes perfectly the power of the tongue. James said: *"If anyone does not stumble in word, he is a perfect man, able to bridle his whole body"* (v. 2 NKJV). Verses 4-5 continue, *"Look also at ships: although they are so large and are driven by fierce winds, they are turned by a very small rudder wherever the pilot desires. Even so the tongue is a little member and boasts great things"* (NKJV). In the same way that a rudder can maneuver a large ship, so our tongue sets a course for our destiny and the one who has control of his tongue is a perfect and wise man.

UNDERSTANDING GOD'S INTENTIONS

In a similar way, blessings work through the power of life that comes from our mouths. Blessing is defined by saying or declaring something to be as God intended for it to be. Blessing is seeing things through prophetic eyes or through the eyes of a seer. It is a matter of moving in the opposite spirit as the accuser or the one who curses. Blessing sees the solution and cursing only reports things as they appear at the moment, or through angry eyes. Blessing magnifies God's intentions for something and cursing magnifies the devil's attempts to open an access point. Blessing calls for Heaven to come to earth and transform a situation. Some have trouble with blessing because they cannot see anything good coming from the person or the situation.

Someone who heard me speak on the power of blessing sent me an email concerning a problem she was having with her boss. She was an office manager, and she felt he was overlooking her for a promotion and an overdue raise. She had not realized she had been cursing her boss. She also discovered she had been inciting others in the office to follow suit. The derogatory statements around the water cooler and at lunch had been well seeded in the office for quite some time. At first, she thought the criticism of the boss was well deserved.

As she read my book, *The Power of Blessing,* she saw how she was actually cursing her redeemer. The one who had created her boss in His image was the one she was aiming her darts at. The Bible teaches us that as we do it to the least, we do it also to Him (Matt. 25:40).

She learned from reading that she needed to clean the office's atmosphere that had become a toxic dumping ground for all things related to the boss, and some had become quite creative with their toxicity. She decided it wouldn't hurt to try it. She arrived at the office before anyone else and started repenting of all that was brought to her mind and her part in leading others to curse. When the office began to buzz with the activity of the day, the usual remarks were flying around like paper airplanes about the mean guy in the other office. She had also learned that she needed to counter the cursing with blessing. She explained to the office staff how she was wrong and apologized to them for her poor leadership regarding the office atmosphere.

This went on for the week, and Friday afternoon she saw the turn-around and was shocked at the results. She was called into the office thinking she be would be fired because it was no secret how she and her boss felt about each other. She entered his office, and with a stern scowl on his face he said, "Shut the door and sit down." He began by repeating how long she had worked there and the job description she had had for a long time. He suddenly apologized to her for withholding the promotion and raise that came with the promotion. He admittedly told of his dislike for her, but something had changed that week. He felt there was peace in the office and on the other employees that had not been there before. He told her "I am going to give you a raise, but it would be retroactive back to the time from a year ago that you should have had the raise and promotion."

She walked out of the office delighted, but it soon sunk in that she had sabotaged what could have been a better environment years before for herself and others on her team. She realized she was to be a thermostat setting the ambiance of the office instead of being the thermometer only registering the frustrations of others and perpetuating the chaos.

In my book, *The Power of Blessing*, I discuss the importance of life-giving communication in marriages. Couples create their marriage by what they say to one another. You have the marriage that you create by the things you speak over your spouse, or we have the marriage we curse. The choice is ours, and it lies in the power of life and death of the tongue.

Christ redeemed all who were under the curse of the law (Gal. 3:13). Since Jesus paid the price with His blood to buy us out of the cursed life Adam fell into; then if you are cursing someone who Christ paid the ultimate price for, you are resisting the work of the cross. The cross was where the curses were nailed. Jesus became the curse for us. He was the scapegoat who took our sin and cursing and removed it from us. If we realized the danger we pose when we are cursing what God has removed the curse from, we would change our minds and repent and come in the same spirit where Christ has set us free.

The picture I have in my mind for those who curse is the Lord pushing the pause button on them, moving forward in favor and blessing. If you want to get off the pause button and push play again, then start right now by repenting for cursing the One who died for the one you are cursing. Now, start blessing by saying what you would like Jesus to say over you. Blessing is not difficult once we see it is speaking over others what you would want Jesus speaking over you. The principle runs all the way through the Bible, which is *"whatever a man sows this he will also reap"* (Gal. 6:7).

YOU GET TO CHOOSE

One benefit of sowing and reaping is we get to determine the fruit or the crop we want to harvest. Any farmer would tell you there is an expectation of what you can grow. If you want to have friends, you must be friendly. If you want to be prosperous, you must be generous.

The second benefit of sowing and reaping is I get to determine the measure of return. Luke 6:38 makes it clear, *"Give, and it will be given to you: good measure, pressed down shaken together, and running over will be put into your bosom. For with the same measure that you use, it will be measured back to you"* (NKJV).

I have learned my prayer can't be one measure and my actions and sowing of another measure. We have been redeemed for abundant life, but for the abundance to become a reality, we need to have our prayer life match up with our real life actions. Some will pray gigantic prayers, and then present a teacup for it to be poured into. If you believed for a million dollars, how would you prepare for it to come to you? The measure we sow is the measure we are preparing for.

Also, this refers to the overflow flowing (Luke 6:38) into your bosom. Some think the bosom is referring to our lap or close in that vicinity. The bosom during the time this was written was referring to an inside pocket of the outer robe many men wore. It would be like a suit jacket pocket today.[2] For someone to pour into the bosom pocket, it would need to be open. For instance, if I am praying for a financial increase, but I never open my bosom pocket to take anything out to give, then my bosom pocket is closed up. Give or open your pocket, and then the pocket will be in a position to receive the overflow. There is a siege on some people financially. A siege is when the enemy surrounds you, and they can't get in, but you can't get out. In the same way, your pocket is under siege because you are not open to give, and thus, you are closed to receive though you are praying for an increase. Giving places your heart in an open position to be able to receive.

THE CIRCUITRY OF HEAVEN

Matthew 18:19 says, *"Again, truly I tell you that if two of you on earth agree about anything they ask for, it will be done for them by my Father in heaven"* (NIV). Let it be on earth as it is in Heaven.

On numerous occasions, my wife, Diane, will be praying and looking at me, she will say "and what do you say?" I know what she is wanting. She wants me to agree with her praying, and I will say, "I agree." Then she will ask what I agree to, and I will need to repeat back to her what I heard her praying. Then we have agreed in word and heart and say "amen" together.

Anyone can agree, but the agreement that brings about change is when you both are seeing and hearing the same thing. The Greek word for agree: (*symphōneō*) means to harmonize as in a music arrangement or to be in the same musical chord.[3] To not agree is to be in discord. The power of agreement when coupled with the agreement of the Holy Spirit is a matchless combination of powerful proportions. Some translations including the King James Version, say agreeing and touching anything it will be done for them. The word for touching (*peri*) means to complete the circuit.[4] The language infers an electrical circuit needs to be completed for the power to be delivered to the right outlet.

First John 5:7-8 tells us: *"There are three that bear witness in heaven: the Father, the Word, and the Holy Spirit; and these are one. And there are three that bear witness on earth: the Spirit, the water, and the blood"* (NKJV). The three in agreement in Heaven are all the titles seen at the dawn of creation. When we agree with what Heaven is declaring, there is a creative anointing released through the circuit of agreement on earth. The witnesses in earth are all elements of redemption and restoration.

The blood brought us near to God through the mediator of His Son. The washing of the water of the word is preparing us for a bridal communion with Him, and the Spirit is giving us instruction on how to approach the throne of grace as an advocate would. So we can see that praying in agreement is more than saying we are in agreement; it connects with the circuitry of Heaven. It is exciting to think we can touch

Heaven. Hebrews 4:15 says He is touched by or sympathizes with the feelings of our infirmities as our High Priest.

When we agree on earth with one another—touching what Heaven is touching—we will see the release of angelic assisted answers. The angel told Daniel in Daniel 10:12, *"From the first day that you set your heart on understanding this and humbling yourself before your God, your words were heard, and I have come in response to your words."* Our words are more powerful than what we know when they are harmonizing with Heaven; then the angels will come who minister on behalf of the heirs of salvation (Heb. 1:14).

We don't have authority to order angels at our beck and call because we were made lower in rank than the angels, but angels are not redeemed like we are. They minister on behalf of us and are submitted to Christ our Redeemer. As a redeemed one, we can touch Heaven with the access of agreement and He who is called the "Captain of the Host" will dispatch His angel army to work together with the heirs of salvation.

The circuitry between Heaven and earth has been bridged through the Lord Jesus Christ. Where Adam broke the circuit between God and man, Jesus—the second Adam—restored the circuitry and communication between Heaven and earth and between God and mankind. First Corinthians 15:47-49 says, *"The first man was of the earth, made of dust; the second Man is the Lord from heaven… And as we have borne the image of the man of dust, we shall also bear the image of the heavenly Man"* (NKJV). Though we still carry traits of the earthly, we also carry the image of the heavenly deep inside our eternal being. When deep calls out to deep (Ps. 42:7), we are communicating with the circuitry of Heaven. Deep inside of our spirit, there is a call that can only be answered by the depths of the heavenly responding in harmony.

In Romans 8:26 we read, *"Likewise the Spirit also helps in our weaknesses. For we do not know what we should pray for as we ought, but the Spirit Himself makes intercession for us with groanings which cannot be uttered"* (NKJV). The Holy Spirit is seen not only giving witness in Heaven but also witnesses in earth. He is praying through us prayers of agreement connecting our spirit to Heaven.

When we feel so inadequate, and at a loss of words, the Spirit of Truth will speak when we give faith to our voice and let Him pray a language that is not of this world and cannot be corrupted or twisted like other known languages. There is no confusion with the Holy Spirit. I don't have to be concerned if something He is praying through me is the will of God. He is part of the witness to the will of God. He is praying exactly the will of God.

Everyone who has been baptized in the Holy Spirit has the witness of the Spirit and the ability to pray outside their abilities and faculties. Sometimes our minds get in the way because of experience in failure and disappointments. The Holy Spirit knows the mind and the will of the Father and will pray accordingly. Hebrews 7:25 tells us that Jesus *"always lives to make intercession"* for us. Jesus told His disciples the Holy Spirit will take what is His and give to them. The Holy Spirit praying through us is part of this circuitry of touching Heaven and earth by taking the intercession of Jesus (John 16:15) and giving it to us, but because our minds could not comprehend the magnitude of this intercession, He needs to pray through us the language of the Spirit.

When we declare what He has already said from His heart, it is a proceeding word. Psalm 107:2 says, *"Let the redeemed of the Lord say so, whom He has redeemed from the hand of the enemy"* (NKJV). The redeemed is agreeing with our Redeemer to bring back what the enemy has stolen. If any two of us is touching our Redeemer, we have what He is saying through us. Without intimacy with Jesus, we never feel the depth of the agreement He has with us. Agreement for the purpose of just getting more stuff is such a shallow understanding of the prayer of agreement. The agreement is to see what He has redeemed to be restored to its original purpose.

THE DIFFERENCE BETWEEN
REDEMPTION AND RESTORATION

Acts 3:19-21 says, *"Repent therefore and be converted, that your sins may be blotted out, so that times of refreshing may come from the presence of the Lord, and that He may send Jesus Christ, who was preached to you before, whom heaven must receive until the times of restoration of all things, which God has spoken by the mouth of all His holy prophets since the world began"* (NKJV).

I have purposely underlined the two places in this verse that refers to times. The Greek uses two different words to describe times; one is *kairos* meaning an open season[5] and *chronos,* which is a set time.[6] The watch you wear can be called a chronometer, so we can conclude chronos is a scheduled time. From this verse, we can see there is always an open time for refreshing or resuscitation. However, there was a set time when Jesus came and became the sacrifice of our redemption.

Galatians 4:2-5 says, *"Until the time [chronos] appointed by the Father... to redeem those who were under the law, that we might receive the adoption as sons"* (NKJV). The time of restoration had begun when the Father sent Jesus to the earth. Not only did redemption occur but also restoration.

Revelation 21:5 He that sat upon the throne said, Behold, I make all things new. Notice it does not say He will make all new things but instead the things He already made will be made new. New in this context deals with putting something back into the original order or design—not a patch job as earlier mentioned, but to its original creation. In Psalm 23, David speaking about the shepherd says, *"He restores my soul."* The Hebrew word here for restore is *shuwb,* which means to return to the beginning or start.

I had a friend who loved old cars—especially the so-called muscle cars of the late 50s and 60s. He would go to a junkyard where cars were salvaged and buy one destined for crushing. He took a rusted out 1957 Chevy Nomad Wagon and spent years and lots of money restoring it to the original from paint down to its original hubcaps. When he agreed to the price the junkyard dealer wanted, he was given a clear Title of Ownership, and he hauled it home to his garage. The day he bought it, he redeemed the car, but the car was not good for anything except scrap. Little by little, he restored the car to not only function as a car, but it was a thing of beauty and workmanship. The value of the car far exceeded its original value. When it was only redeemable, no one wanted the rust bucket; but once it was restored, everyone noticed it and my friend could name his price.

For many of us, when Jesus redeemed us from the curse of humanity, we received a clear title to be born again, but dreams and hopes of the future were not yet seen. I am glad He sees in us far more than we see in ourselves. Our value is not based on where we came from but based on the price He paid with His own blood. He gave us the Holy Spirit to help restore us to God's original intent. He didn't save us so we would remain in the junkyard of life. He saw the beauty of His creation to be restored.

In Jeremiah 18:4, Jeremiah was told by the Lord to go down to the potter's house. A potter at that time was a very skilled and important person. They made most of the utensils for the house. In verses 3-4 we read, *"I went down to the potter's house, and there he was, making something at the wheel. And the vessel that he made of clay was marred in the hand of the potter, so he made it again into another vessel, as it seemed good to the potter to make"* (NKJV). The vessel in his hand was not usable, and the imperfections lowered the value or perhaps the vessel with cracks would leak. Instead of throwing it away he made it again.

Paul says if any are in Christ, they are a new creation (2 Cor. 5:17). They are made new based on the original intent of the creator. Romans 9:20-21 says something similar but more direct: *"Will the thing formed say to him who formed it, 'Why have you made me like this?' Does not the potter have power over the clay, from the same lump to make one vessel for honor and another for dishonor"* (NKJV). Not only did He come to save us but also to restore us to be a vessel of honor not just functionality. The frustration some people have is dealing with the potter. They want to order what He does or decide what they are to be. This verse flies in the face of those who try to make the case that God made a mistake on their gender preference. Paul stated clearly it's the power of the potter over the clay questioning the potter as to why he made you like this. The problem with the clay is it does not trust the outcome of the potter's restoration process. Like my friend restoring the old rusted heap, it was a process and, at times, when the paint was stripped off and parts removed, the car looked worse than it did in the junkyard, but eventually it came together, and the results were amazing.

Second Timothy 2:20-21 tells us, *"In a great house there are not only vessels of gold and silver, but also of wood and clay, some for honor and some for dishonor. Therefore if anyone cleanses himself from the latter, he will be a vessel for honor, sanctified and useful for the Master, prepared for every good work"* (NKJV).

In every Jewish house at that time, there were at least seven basic vessels used for various household tasks. Each vessel had a specific function for the daily use of the house. Some vessels came from earthen materials, and some came from costly gold or silver that was refined several times to get the purest of gold. The two main vessel categories were divided into honor and dishonor. A vessel of dishonor was one used for human waste or garbage. The vessels of honor were those used exclusively for drinking or the master's use.[8]

Paul is writing to a young protégé who was a pastor saying if anyone cleanses himself and wants to be a vessel of honor, let him be sanctified. Sanctified means to be set apart for exclusive use. For instance, you wouldn't use your toothbrush to clean the toilet. Your toothbrush is set aside for the exclusive use to be put in your mouth.

Redemption leads us to restoration not just being a redeemed vessel but a vessel that has been cleansed and set aside for holy use. The Holy Spirit in all of us knows the plan the Father has to restore us to His original intent and use. The Spirit of Truth will guide us toward restoration, and it may even look like a complete makeover, but it's His original design.

NOT A PATCHED-UP VERSION

Jesus is using two parables to explain the process of restoration. Luke 5:36 tells us, *"No one puts a piece from a new garment on an old one; otherwise the new makes a tear, and also the piece that was taken out of the new does not match the old"* (NKJV) The application relates to us as an old garment. Taking a new piece to patch an old garment only makes the tear worse in the garment. The message is that God doesn't just patch us up with a little bit of new and a whole lot of the old past.

Here is the next parable in verses 37-38, *"No one puts new wine into old wineskins; or else the new wine will burst the wineskins and be spilled, and the wineskins will be ruined. But new wine must be put into new wineskins, and both are preserved"* (NKJV). The culture of that time understood these examples. Everyone knew that new wine would ferment and expand, and if the wineskins were not flexible and ready to expand, they would burst. The process of restoring wineskins was extensive.

They did not throw away the wineskin; it was redeemed and then restored. The badger skin was turned the wrong side out and scraped with a piece of broken pottery to remove the sediment left from the former contents. The skin was soaked in a solution of our equivalent of homemade lye soap. The skin was hand washed and scraped a second time. The skin was allowed to dry, and then a concoction of olive oil and other types of oil were hand rubbed until the skin was saturated and pliable. Now that the skin was restored like new, it was ready for the new wine moving and expanding inside the skin.[9]

God's plan of salvation not only includes being saved out of darkness and sin but to restore us to the plan God had for man before Adam fell from God's original intent. He wants to fill us with the New Wine of the Spirit and be flexible with the moving of the Spirit inside of us. You are a new creation, not a patched-up barely surviving son or daughter of the King. Allow Him to place you on the potter's wheel and give Him the trust and freedom to reform and transform you into His design so you will be a vessel of honor.

Lord Jesus, we are asking You today to help us to be aware of the power You have invested in us and that we would be wise stewards of this authority. Make us conscious of what comes out of our mouth and to be sowers of life especially among our spouses and family. We want to be in partnership with Heaven to bring about Your counsel on earth. We are ready for the reforming of any area of our life that needs to have restoration so we would be a vessel ready for use. I ask that those reading these pages would find hope to move past a season of stagnation and disappointment. We are ready and willing for the New Wine of Your Spirit to be poured in and that we would be carriers of Your glory. Amen!

CHAPTER 8

DEVELOPING THE SEER IN YOU

SPIRITUAL DEVELOPMENT IS an important topic when it comes to pursuing, overtaking, and recovering. In the last three chapters, we will discuss developing the seer, the sayer, and the doer in you. All these areas of development allow you to not only mature spiritually but make you more effective in seeing restoration in your family, your workplace, and in every part of your life where you connect with God and people.

The word "seer" is normally understood as an Old Testament word for a prophet. The seer would travel from town to town and mostly prophesy to kings. We don't see the word used in the New Testament as such. I use the word seer not as a prophetic term only but under-standing—seeing—what God is doing.

In John 5:19, Jesus said, *"Most assuredly, I say to you, the Son can do nothing of Himself, but what He sees the Father do; for whatever He does, the Son also does in like manner"* (NKJV). Jesus was aware at all times what was transpiring in the spiritual realm as well as the polit-ical agendas of His day. Some would try to pull Jesus into discussions concerning the hatred of the Roman occupation. Jesus simply said, *"Render to Caesar the things that are Caesar's and to God the things that are God's*" (Mark 12:17). He was aware of their treatment at the hands of the Romans, but kept His affections on things above; perhaps this is why miracles were happening wherever He went due to seeing what the Father had in store.

I don't limit the seer to only seeing with physical eyes. It may be through a thought that casts an image or picture in your mind. In any case, you see something no matter the mode in which it appears to you. Like any gift we receive from the Lord, it must be filtered through the absolute, inerrant Word of God. Obviously, not every thought picture passing through the corridors of our mind is sent from Heaven. They possibly could be natural thoughts we should give attention to, but not necessarily something that affects everyone or should be brought into a corporate arena for attention. Seers who are always sounding the alarm to draw attention to their gift or ministry will lose credibility with the larger gathering of intercessors.

SEEING FOR YOUR FAMILY

Several years ago I was awakened in the middle of the night with an urgency to pray for our son, Kevin. Kevin was touring the United States and other countries with the band he had started. They were enjoying moderate success and were signed with a national label. They traveled extensively, and so I was not always aware of their location, as they would play concerts almost every night while touring. On this particular night, I could see death was hovering around him. Not having any details, I prayed for their safety and protection. I prayed for a long period until I felt the urgency had passed.

The next morning, I called Kevin, and when he answered, I immediately said, "Kevin, what is going on?" Normally, it would have been a casual update kind of conversation. He could tell from my voice I was matter-of-fact. He said, "What do you mean?" I said, "I was up in the middle of the night last night praying for your safety." He didn't want to worry me, but he knew that if the Holy Spirit aroused me to pray, I was not going to stop till I knew the situation.

He told me of what I saw vaguely. They had a touring bus, and every night they took turns sleeping on the bus and the other half of the band would stay in a hotel. That particular night, Kevin was sleeping on the bus when sometime during the night an eighteen wheeler pulled up next to them and left the diesel engine running all night as they normally would do. But because the truck was parked so close to them, the bus began filling with carbon monoxide fumes and exhaust. Kevin and the others on the bus were not able to awaken themselves to get out.

The bus driver was staying in the hotel but was awakened and remembered something he felt he needed to get out of the bus. When he opened the door of the bus, he could smell the deadly gas had consumed the oxygen and he was able to drag them outside and get them into fresh air.

My redemptive relationship with the Holy Spirit had given me a sensitivity to pay attention to what I am seeing. In this case, I was awakened, then I saw how I needed to pray. Being a seer is closely connected to understanding the covenant (*Secret Power of Covenant* book) which is an intimate connection to knowing the Holy Spirit will keep me alert and in the loop of what I need to know to be a partner in His kingdom.

In First Chronicles 12:32, we are told about the Issachar tribe. The sons of Issachar were about two hundred leaders from the Tribe of Issachar. They were given the ability to understand the political and spiritual condition of Israel and the wisdom to know how to respond. They were aware of the prophetic destiny for their nation and followed the transitions and transformation from one king to another. These could be said to be a type of seers, not because of carrying the position of a national prophet, but because they were the type of intercessors who knew not only the assessment of the problem but how to pray and call others to pray.

Today, we need those who are seers who carry this anointing as these special men of Issachar did for their nation. Seers are needed to be part of the restoration of all that the Lord has redeemed. The United States for generations has been called a Christian nation. Our history is rich with leaders who carried the spiritual calling to see what God wanted the nation to do. It wasn't about their influence with presidents and political dignitaries but their influence to call others into seeking God and repenting over the sins of the nation. Second Chronicles 7:14 declares that if the people of God repented, God would heal the land. It was not calling for certain people in our government to repent and acknowledge the sins of the nation; it was the people of the nation.

Sons of Issachar anointing will see the plots and plans of the enemy and gain supernatural strategy of how to intercede. The true influencers are those who will see the true issues facing our nation and will not be distracted by political and media filters but will set their heart to seek God. Their influence goes much higher than any political office or position held by man; (Eph. 2:6) they are seated in the heavenly position.

Their wisdom does not come from the wisdom of man but from God. James 3:17 tells us, *"The wisdom that is from above is first pure, then peaceable, gentle, willing to yield, full of mercy and good fruits, without partiality and without hypocrisy"* (NKJV). Carrying wisdom from God is also knowing how to apply the wisdom given. The application must be administrated with peace and gentleness as to not alienate those who will follow you.

I see the United States once again gaining new strength due to the seers prophesying the heart of God for restoration. There are always those who call for judgment to come to America, but true seers understand that is not God's will to bring judgment but to bring restoration.

Redemption was paid for with His Son's blood, so restoration is His first choice. Seers can stand in the place of intercession and preempt judgment. James 2:13 says, *"For judgment will be merciless to one who has shown no mercy; mercy triumphs over judgment."* Seers are not called to herald judgment but to cry out for mercy and to influence others to understand the timing of the Lord and the season we are in. Gifted seers are able to see the larger plan so they won't get bogged down in one season. Seasons are passages toward a greater destiny.

When I talk about a seer, I'm talking about the ability to see what God sees. It is very similar to the word "truth," *alētheia ,* which means the manifested the reality through God's eyes.[1] *"When the Spirit of Truth comes, he will guide you into all truth"* (John 16:13 NLT). Being a "truth seer" is not the same as being a "flesh seer;" in fact, it is the opposite.

Seeing as God does is seeing the potential of restoration in people. We don't naturally have this quality in us; it needs to be developed. Rather than voicing a negative opinion about the service at a restaurant, or the seating choice, a seer changes the atmosphere. Developing a "seer grace" allows us to see what God is doing or what God wants to say or do in that environment. We can change an environment from one that is caustic to one filled with spiritual sensitivity. The environment can affect how people hear what the Lord is saying. Part of developing a seer anointing is to know how to change the atmosphere you are in. In some places, there may be a deaf and dumb spirit that is disruptive for anyone to really hear the depth of what you are saying. The seed you are sowing is good, but the ground is not receiving it.

I found myself in a difficult environment as I was invited to speak at a church I had not been to before. The worship was lukewarm, and it appeared as if most were robotic. My first thought was "why did I come because I could be doing other things that would be a better use of my time?" I struggled along for the first ten minutes trying to find a point of life I could connect with. I heard the Holy Spirit say "sing to them" I thought, "I am not a singer," and I saw how they were worshipping and they didn't seem to enjoy it. I continued to be prompted, and as I shut my eyes and focused on singing unto the Lord a spontaneous song; I let loose with a song that was of intimacy between the bride and the bridegroom. I got lost in the moment, and I didn't seem to mind being there any longer. I opened my eyes to see others weeping with lifted hands broken by the sweet presence of the Lord. The atmosphere had changed, and I was able to move into the message that lead to personal ministry. That day I learned how important it was to be able to see the atmosphere as well as the message needed.

In Mark 6:2-5, Jesus came into Nazareth where He had grown up as a young boy. On the Sabbath, he entered the synagogue teaching, and many were astonished at the wisdom and revelation in which He taught them. They couldn't get past their familiarity with Him; remembering the time when He was just a boy playing in the streets. His family was still there, and so they were offended that He was not like them. In verse 4,

Jesus said, *"A prophet is not without honor except in his own country."* He continued in verse 5, *"He could do no mighty work there, except that He laid His hands on a few sick people and healed them"* (NKJV).

This verse drives home my point on how important an atmosphere is. Jesus, the Son of God, was restricted due to the lack of honor. The environment sets the tone for what can be done. Though there may be willing hearts, there also must be honoring the anointing in that place. The word for honor is also translated as glory. Where there is no welcoming in the presence of God, there is no manifestation of His Glory. If restoration is to take place, the atmosphere must be prepared to eliminate the toxicity of any unforgiveness or spiritual pride.

In First Samuel 16:7, God sent Samuel to anoint the new king who would take King Saul's place. Samuel saw the first son, Eliab, a strong strapping son of Jesse. On appearance, he looked like good kingly material, but God said this is not the one. In verse 7 we read, *"The Lord said to Samuel 'Do not look at his appearance or at his physical stature, because I have refused him; for the Lord does not see as man sees; for man looks at the outward appearance but the Lord looks at the heart'"* (NKJV).

After seven sons had passed in front of Samuel; he asked Jesse if he has any other sons. Well, the smallest one is out in the field tending to sheep. When David was brought before Samuel, God said that's the man.

What we perceive can deceive. When our perception is based only on natural conditions and sightings, we can miss the most important spiritual reality. One of the most important cautions for seers is to learn the difference between natural perception and spiritual revelation.

I have a friend who prophesies by perception. He looks for something familiar to prompt the flow. For instance, they see someone with a football jersey with the number 12, which triggers biblical numbers and 12 is the number of government, then they give them a word about governing. This is risky due to relying on natural senses to see rather than spiritual eyes that see. I am not saying this may not work, but if we lean on this only, it can become a crutch and the dependency on this will weaken the development of deeper revelations.

For example, if God says you are going to raise the dead and you've never raised the dead, what He said to you is not nullified by what you haven't done. Prophecy is a proceeding word. It is a word moving in a forward direction. It's a catalyst to move us from where we are to where we're going. And many times that word doesn't come about until we are prepared to start seeing the opportunities.

NEED TO KNOW BASIS

A lady approached me at the end of the service one Sunday morning. She said to me, "I know you know."

"What is it I'm supposed to know that you think I know?"

She said, "I know God speaks to you and you know."

I was getting confused about what I was supposed to know. She finally started unraveling the puzzle for me. She had assumed I discerned she had a problem with drug addiction. She was an older lady who was always kind and somewhat reserved. I was actually shocked she was dealing with anything of the sort. I assured her I was not aware of her difficulty. I am not sure if she was disappointed in me that I did not see that in her. But I told her that being a seer is on a need to know basis. If I don't need to know something, the Holy Spirit does not open the eyes of my heart to see anything. She asked again what I meant. "God never says anything to me unless I need to know it. So whatever you think I know about you, the Holy Spirit did not think I needed to know it."

WHAT IS IN A NAME?

God's not uncovering you to people. He doesn't expose you to people who have no need or business knowing things about you. The purpose of being able to see something is to enact a solution over the issue seen—not for the purpose of uncovering anyone.

Many times the Spirit will give you a name to identify the situation thereby gaining authority over it by naming it. Let me explain. In Genesis 2:19, we see the account of creation whereby the animals were created: *"Out of the ground the Lord God formed every beast of the field and every bird of the air, and brought them to Adam to see what he would call them. And whatever Adam called each living creature, that was its name"* (NKJV).

Notice that God wanted to see what name Adam would give each animal. Adam was given authority and everything he named he had authority over. We give names to diseases which gives us authority over what we name. When the devil tries to place another name on you as to gain control; you as a seer can counter that name by blessing yourself with the name God says about you as a son or daughter of the Most High God.

Nicknames can stick to us to create an alternate destiny or picture of who we are. As a seer, you might see the problem and be given a name for that issue so you can take dominion over it. Perhaps you have heard of instances where someone was called shorty or stubby or some other trait that was unbecoming to who you are. Those labels can stick and create images of oneself that follow them the rest of their life. Proverbs 23:7 says, *"As he thinks in his heart so is he"* (NKJV).

Names can create pictures and pictures can create destinies. For instance, the Holy Spirit may let you see someone, and give you a name for him or her. The name is not for the purpose to tell them they should change their birth certificate, but for the purpose of praying over them that particular name. The military assign names to certain missions such as "operation desert storm" and everyone who hears the name immediately knows how to respond. The enemy does not get to name the mission—we do. If you have been labeled a derogatory name; allow the Holy Spirit to rename you for the purpose of your mission. Names qualify for anointing just like military missions with code names qualify for funding, equipment, and certain levels of ranking in authority that is unique to that code name.

In the beginning, God wanted to partner with us, and God never gives up on His plan. He doesn't alter his plan or change his mind. Today, He's still seeking a partnership with us. And if He can get us to see what He sees, then we name the situation as Adam did and take dominion over the issue.

PERSPECTIVE AND PERCEPTION

If you see a problem and you don't see it from God's perspective, your natural senses will name it and give it more power than it deserves.

Whatever you give power to, you become subject to it—even to the point where you feel out of control. For instance, some might say; "I have no hope of ever getting out of this trouble." Seers are careful of their conversations as to not give dominion to the enemy who attempts to give us another perspective on the situation.

The Bible says, *"Trust in the Lord with all your heart and do not lean on your own understanding. In all your ways acknowledge Him, and He will make your paths straight"* (Prov. 3:5-6). To lean on our understanding can depend on the perspective or angle in which I am viewing something. One can form a quick first impression based on past experience when the situation you are viewing has nothing to do with your experience. Our past can position us to see out of offenses or personal experience with rejection. A seer must have a clear palate to taste something fresh to not taint what God wants you to see.

> *"The hand of the Lord was on me, and he brought me out by the Spirit of the Lord and set me in the middle of a valley; it was full of bones. He led me back and forth among them, and I saw a great many bones on the floor of the valley, bones that were very dry. He asked me, 'Son of man, can these bones live?' I said, 'Sovereign Lord, you alone know'"* (Ezek. 37:1-3 NIV).

God gives Ezekiel a vision in which he is right in the middle of a valley filled with dry, dead bones. The bones are symbolic of Israel and where they are at that point in history. God asks him if what he saw—bones—could become living people again. Ezekiel didn't know, answering that only God alone knew the answer. He wanted Ezekiel to see from His perspective the condition of the nation. Based on what you see, can these bones live? God wasn't asking him what he saw in the natural, but what he saw in the spiritual realm. Once Ezekiel was seeing from God's perspective, he was released to prophesy.

*Then he said to me, "Speak a prophetic message to these bones
and say, 'Dry bones, listen to the word of the Lord! This is what
the Sovereign Lord says: Look! I am going to put breath into you
and make you live again! I will put flesh and muscles on you
and cover you with skin. I will put breath into you, and you will
come to life. Then you will know that I am the Lord.'" So I spoke
this message, just as he told me. Suddenly as I spoke, there was a
rattling noise all across the valley. The bones of each body came
together and attached themselves as complete skeletons. Then as
I watched, muscles and flesh formed over the bones. ... 'Come, O
breath, from the four winds! Breathe into these dead bodies so
they may live again.'" So I spoke the message as he commanded
me, and breath came into their bodies. They all came to life and
stood up on their feet—a great army* (Ezekiel 37:4-10 NLT).

FIRST IMPRESSIONS

One of the first lessons of growing into a seeing grace is not to
be moved by your first impressions. We have certain personalities
we're drawn to, and there are certain personalities we stay away from.
Someone who has an arrogant personality walks into a room with an
attitude, "Hi, here I am. You were no doubt looking for me and waiting
for me to get here. You're so fortunate that I'm here." When I encounter
that type of person, something in me wants to rise up and say, "Sit down
and shut up." It would be wrong for me to say that, obviously. But certain personalities cause us to draw back.

But first impressions aren't always the best thing to base our percep-
tions on—whether a person or a situation. It is wrong to look at what

a person is wearing and then base what kind of person he or she is on their taste in clothes. God may have done an amazing transformation in that person's life, and there may be an exciting testimony—but when we assume and prejudge, we nullify any opportunity to see what God has for them based on the blockage of the first impression.

God was telling Ezekiel that if he saw what God saw, he could prophesy to the people and believe by faith for something that he didn't believe would happen. Think about that. If we give a word, we really don't believe by faith; we're just appeasing the ears. But if we can see what He sees, then we can prophesy, and things will begin to change for the better from that point.

Psalm 27:13 says, *"I would have lost heart, unless I had believed that I would see the goodness of the Lord in the land of the living"* (NKJV).

Unless we have the right understanding of redemption and ultimately restoration, we can lose heart. Losing heart has to do with passion and motivation. One may have a vision for something but lack motivation to pursue because he won't be able to overcome and recover all. There must be the ability to see the goodness in the face of disaster or disappointment. Remember, disappointment is simply a preconceived idea that was not God's originally. We become disappointed when things didn't work out the way we wanted, but it may be premature to lose heart because the timing has not fully come or others connected to the answer are not yet in place for all the pieces to come together.

Keeping the passion alive comes by focusing on the Lord and the land or places He has blessed you in. Think back to all the times you saw breakthrough and enjoyed a victory. David no doubt thought of how the Lord delivered the lion and the bear into his hands while watching his father's sheep. If God did it for you, then He will do it now in the land of your living. Part of the tactic of the enemy is to get us to question God's plan. The serpent posed the question to Adam's wife; "has God said" leaving the thought that maybe I misunderstood what He was saying.

The key to keeping heart was that we could "Believe to see." Losing sight of what I believe to see is cause for losing my motivation. Anyone who is successful at anything will attest to all the obstacles and discouragements they had to hurdle before seeing what they truly believed for.

Acts 3:2 says, *"A certain man lame from his mother's womb was carried whom they laid daily at the gate of the temple, which is called Beautiful to ask alms from those who enter the temple"* (NKJV). The significance of this account of a paralyzed man at the temple gate perhaps is more telling than at first glance. The writer goes into detail to give us the setting at the gate near the temple called Beautiful. This name is translated (*hōraios*) meaning the right timing or the right season.[2]

Obviously, the man had been there for many years, and most who frequented the temple knew of him. After the upper room experience, Peter and John are going to the temple to pray. This time they see the man different than they had before they were filled with the Holy Spirit. The man was at the gate of "Right Timing," and the miracle took place for his healing and transformation.

Before redemption, there was no expectation of restoration. After redemption the eyes of those who had encountered the Holy Spirit were now seeing the paralytic with more than sympathy; they are viewing this man with eyes of a seer with restoration in mind. Peter is so confident that he pulls the man up as to say "I am not taking no for an answer."

Though this poor paralyzed man thought it was just another day with perhaps hope of receiving a few alms or the portion normally allotted to beggars; instead, he had a suddenly. A suddenly can be defined as this; when the promise of God intersects with the timing of God, there is a suddenly. The gifting of seers is able to know the times and promises to release an act of faith resulting in a suddenly.

"Faith is the substance of things hoped for" (Heb. 11:1 NKJV). Hope is the ability to see beauty from the ash pile, and hope will keep faith moving forward. Hope is not wishful thinking; hope is an expectation that's born of the Spirit of God and is often called the anchor of the soul.

John 11:1-44 tells the story of Jesus raising Lazarus from the dead. Lazarus' sisters sent word to Jesus to come and heal their brother. They assumed Jesus would immediately come to Bethany. Instead, *"Jesus said this sickness is not unto death but for the glory of God, that the Son may be glorified through it"* (John 11:4 NKJV). Jesus stayed two more days before going to Bethany. When Jesus arrived, there was weeping and disappointment that Jesus had not arrived sooner.

Jesus wept but not for the same reason they were. Jesus wept at the lack of faith He saw. They did not take Him at His word *"that the sickness is not unto death."* They knew Jesus as one who heals, but they did not know Him as the resurrection and life. They perceived the situation as finished; Jesus had already seen Lazarus as being raised. Those who saw their brother and friend as dead were grieving. They only saw Him as healer and were limited when the time of healing had passed.

Let me inject this point; seers can save themselves grief if they confine themselves to the word they have not the circumstances they are feeling by their surroundings. The way we see Jesus our Redeemer is the level we can move in faith. In some cases, it may seem like the opportunity for success has passed and it's easy for grief to set in; but remember, you are at the "Gate of Right Timing" not the gate of despair. You won't faint or become weak in faith if you continue to stand for your Land of Living.

FROM GLORY TO GLORY

Ecclesiastes 7:8 says, *"The end of a matter is better than it's begin-ning…."* Although He can give us the ability to see how something will end, we still have to go all the way through the process. I like what a friend of mine says, "The Bible says we're moving from glory to glory, but there's hell in the hallway." So we keep our hearts set upon the glory while passing through moments of transition—when we don't neces-sarily know what's going on. We just know the end will result in seeing the glory of God in the matter.

Many years ago, when I was a single father, raising three children alone, I was returning from Africa with a stopover in London. I had an encounter with the Lord that evening and the small room where I was resting suddenly filled with light, and I couldn't look up. In a matter of seconds, the Lord said to my spirit that I was going to be tested, my family was going to be sifted like wheat and to pray that your faith doesn't fail. That's what He told Peter, too. And then He said, "You will not hear from Me for a while, but know that I haven't left you."

For more than three years, when I read my Bible, it was like reading a dry novel. I got nothing out of it. I would pray, and felt nothing. But

I remembered the last thing He said to me, "I won't be with you for a while, but after you've come through this wilderness, you will come out of this wilderness in the power of My Spirit." I knew this was a make or break moment for my family and me. I didn't understand the process, but I knew my Redeemer lived and that because He lived, I would see something better at the end than I saw at the moment.

Though at times I felt abandoned by some I thought were friends for life, it was a time that I needed to walk out alone. I knew there was no sin connected to the testing, and I knew my family would stand with me. For the three years, I kept pressing forward—sometimes out of sheer discipline and no emotional motivation. I had no family living within five hundred miles, yet I knew in my heart that God was near though His promises were concealed (Prov. 25:2) at the moment and my job was to seek out those promises He had spoken in the past and contend for the fullness of them.

Then, one day just as suddenly as the testing came, so did the breaking of the silence come! While driving, the Holy Spirit said: "It's time to come out of the wilderness, but you will come out in the power of the Spirit." I recognized the verse from Jesus being tested in Luke 4:14. He told me I was to accept an invitation from a local church I had been turning down due to losing the desire to preach anymore. I had become comfortable just raising my children and trying to be the best father possible. When I seemed resistant, the Holy Spirit repeated the instructions with one caveat, "If you choose not to obey, you will be in rebellion to me." This got my attention, and I quickly obeyed. I can tell you today the ending of the testing resulted in a greater weight of glory. I learned to stay with being a seer of the Lord's goodness in the land of my living even though circumstances were not confirming it.

HOPE DEFERRED

Proverbs 13:12 says, *"Hope deferred makes the heart sick, but when the desire comes, it is tree of life"* (NKJV). When hope is founded on the basis of faith, it will have times of the heart feeling weak. But when the end of the testing comes, the tree of life springs back, and you soon forget the sick heart and the joy that is set before becomes life-sustaining.

Learning to deal with your feelings as a seer is of utmost importance. Your feelings or emotions can drive us in a wrong direction all the while feeling you are correct. Other people who don't carry the same seer anointing can add to the fueled misguided emotions. In flying, it's called vertigo. Vertigo is when you are upside down, but it seems you are flying right side up. The old school flyers used the term "flying by the seat of your pants." This term has been used for various explanations—especially to describe one as not sure of what they are doing. The term was first coined as dealing with vertigo. The early flyers who didn't have today's electronics went by the sense that if they were upside down, they could not feel the weight on their bottom, then they were in vertigo, but if they could feel their weight in the seat, then they were all right with gravity. Though feelings can be deceiving, none of us would want to live life so sterile that we had no emotional fortitude at all.

Worship without passion is just another song service. So, how can we live with emotions without letting them be the GPS of our life? First off, emotions should not give us direction, but after we know the way, then emotions can play a vital role in stimulating forward progress and attracting others to join the team. David made a declaration in Psalm 84:2 saying, *"My heart and my flesh cry out for the living God"* (NKJV). We can actually train our flesh to be more compliant through worship.

In worship, we involve all three components of our life: body, soul, and spirit. The more we subject our feelings and emotions to engage in worship, the less distracted we become.

Whatever we feed, lives whether in the physical or the spiritual. If the emotions are fed a diet of distrust and gossip, the soul becomes unstable and can swing like a pendulum. James 1:8 says, *"A double minded man is unstable in all of his ways"* (KJV). Those who lead others must have their direction consistently unwavering. The instability in leaders makes it difficult for others to duplicate or follow. When there is instability, the end result of restoration can be slowed down or delayed, and in some cases, another visionary will need to pick up the challenge and move forward.

DELAYED BUT DENIED

In First Samuel 1:11, you will recount the history of Hannah and her husband Elkanah. Elkanah had two wives. Hannah bore no children, and in that culture, she could be considered dishonoring and even cursed to not produce children. Elkanah's second wife was Peninnah who bore children. The rivalry for the attention of their husband perhaps was painful for Hannah.

Verse 6 says, *"And her rival also provoked her severely, to make her miserable, because the Lord had closed her womb"* (NKJV). While waiting for a suddenly to take place, the enemy delights in harassing us through use of comparison. I can just see Peninnah saying to Hannah on the way to the temple to worship; "Hey Hannah, where are your babies?" but the truth was Hannah would be the carrier for the greatest prophet of the nation.

By all outward appearances, Hannah was barren, but with eyes of redemption, she is carrying the seed of the deliverer. She was not being denied a son, only delayed to bring Hannah to the point of releasing her son into the service of the Lord.

Eli, the priest, had become old, and no longer had any discipline or control over his sons. The sons were to serve in the temple in very strict structural areas of service. Instead, they were sleeping with the women who were to sacrifice their offerings to the Lord (2:22). Due to the blatant sin swirling around the priestly ministry, people were crying out to God, and open vision was shut in Shiloh, and the nation was without any prophetic revelation (3:1).

There are times when the timing is as crucial as receiving the word. God wanted to cleanse the nation of the corruption that came through Eli and his sons. When the time came, and Samuel was placed in the temple to learn the voice of the Lord; in one day, God purged the temple. Eli's sons were killed in battle, and Eli after hearing the news, fell backward and broke his neck. Hannah went on to have other children, and God greatly blessed her with favor.

First Corinthians 4:5 says, *"Judge nothing before the time, until the Lord come, who will both bring to light the hidden things of darkness and reveal the counsels of the hearts. Then each one's praise will come from God"* (NKJV). First impressions are not the best discerner of what God is doing, and for some seers, they will endure ridicule until the time comes when what they have been hoping for had finally come to light. When passing through transitional times, remember what He has said to you in the beginning. He hasn't changed His mind. Circumstances around you and what people say may change, but the Word of the Lord is, "Yes, and amen forever, forever, and ever or let it be set and established in heaven!" He says.

TEMPORARY VERSUS ETERNAL

Second Corinthians 4:18 says, *"So we don't look at the troubles we can see now; rather, we fix our gaze on things that cannot be seen. For the things we see now will soon be gone, but the things we cannot see will last forever"* (NLT). The things we can see only with our spiritual seer eyes are eternal. The things we see with our natural senses are temporary, and if we get locked into the temporary, we lose the ability to see the unseen—the eternal. Sometimes we can't see what God is doing in a bigger way because we're so locked in and grieving over the momentary issues that come and go as often as the weather changes.

We get so upset because of some little issue that has no bearing on where we want to go. Instead, we must keep our spiritual eyes, hearts, minds, and spirits gazing toward the end goal. Jesus could have been overwhelmed by the crowd yelling, "Crucify Him; Crucify Him." He could have been so upset because of the friend who sat at the table and ate bread and drank wine with Him, all the while knowing Judas would betray Him. But Jesus set His heart and His affection upon the weightier things, the eternal things.

"...Let us run with endurance the race that is set before us, fixing our eyes on Jesus, the author and perfecter of faith, who for the joy set before Him endured the cross, despising the shame, and has sat down at the right hand of the throne of God" (Heb. 12:1-2).

The joy that set before Jesus was not the cross but the conclusion of the plan of redemption when He would once again sit at the right hand of His Father. Jesus was able to keep His heart upon the ultimate joy and not get sidetracked with the process of getting to the end.

THREE SEER DEVELOPMENT POINTS

The following are three ways to develop the seer grace in you:

1. Look beyond the obvious and see what would glorify God as an outcome. We all have the Word of God to refer to when we want to know what God really wants us to do. Keep in mind that God doesn't want you to fail. We know God doesn't want us to be disappointed in Him and He wants to be glorified. So we have to see the desired outcome when taking action or making decisions. What about this outcome would glorify God the most? For instance, if I believe for a promotion, I can develop the seeing grace by setting a goal to glorify God through the promotion. Pray in the same vein you are seeing as if it was already completed and the answer is in process.

2. Develop a wholesome filter in your heart. Philippians 4:8 says, *"Fix your thoughts on what is true, and honorable, and right, and pure, and lovely, and admirable. Think about things that are excellent and worthy of praise"* (NLT). That is how you develop a wholesome perspective so that you can filter out what you see in the world around you. We must not be disrespectful to others who happen not to share our view. What we behold we become. Be aware of where your focus has been set upon.

3. Spend time daily meditating upon key verses and rehearsing them in prayer. Since faith comes by hearing; being able to hear yourself will strengthen your resolve to finish strong. Find those of like mind and fellowship with those who can help develop your spiritual senses. Hebrews 5:14 tells us our senses are skillful by reason of use. Any gift we use causes us to be aware of the opportunity to engage the gift. Start at home by seeing what the family is lacking and set your eyes to pray the solution not the problem.

THE WRONG VIEW

1. Number one is being suspicious of others and having a vain imagination that works against you. The devil knows how to push our buttons to cause a negative reaction, so we will enter into a battle with someone over something trivial. Save your strength for the real battles. Don't fight battles the Holy Spirit has not led you into which is the good fight of faith all others are pseudo shadow boxing.

2. Number two is being disappointed. When we have an assumption or presumption that God was going to move in a particular way at a particular time, and He didn't, our soul becomes weak, and we become discouraged and disappointed. Disappointment can be self-centered and will only serve to delay unnecessarily. Return to the place of resting in the fact that you have already heard and do not let the devil abort the seed. Water the seed daily and give thanks for the completion.

3. Number three is the lack of worship. The third way we can lose sight and adopt a wrong view is to stop worshiping Him. Psalm 16:11 says in the presence of the Lord *"there is fullness of joy"* and at His right hand there *"are pleasures forevermore."* (ESV). Worship is the restoring of the soul. It replenishes the battle fatigue that comes after a prolonged time of resistance. Know when to cease fighting and enter into refreshing.

Your strength comes from the Lord, not any other outside source. Others can give encouragement but not strength. Encouragement is short lived until the next arrow flies. Strength is the inner spirit being resuscitated by the breath of the Spirit ministering to you. Jesus had times when He would get alone, and the ministry of the Spirit would come. When I make time to be with Him, to enter into His presence and love Him, it's amazing how clear and easy I can hear.

Now when the attendant of the man of God had risen early and gone out, behold, an army with horses and chariots was circling the city. And his servant said to him, "Alas, my master! What shall we do?" So he answered, "Do not fear, for those who are with us are more than those who are with them." Then Elisha prayed and said, "O Lord, I pray, open his eyes that he may see." And the Lord opened the servant's eyes and he saw; and behold, the mountain was full of horses and chariots of fire all around Elisha (2 Kings 6:15-17).

I ask Father that You open every reader's eyes to see how our Redeemer has called us to serve as a seer. I pray for the spirit of truth to be upon you, for the lies of the enemy to be silenced and destroyed. I pray you will not lose heart or faith or confidence. I pray you would have the right perspective and always be able to see what the Father is doing. May the Lord grant a sense of spiritual timing and wisdom in how to apply each season you are passing through. Today is the day you will think and see clearly because you carry the seed to partner with the Holy Spirit to accomplish great things in your family. Whatever you are asking for; extend your faith beyond what you can ask or even think. Amen!

CHAPTER 9

DEVELOPING THE HEARER IN YOU

DEVELOPING THE ABILITY to hear begins with understanding what is meant by hearing. Hearing in Scripture goes beyond listening. One can listen but not understand.

My fifth grade math class was a listening class, but not an understanding class. That year they introduced what was called new math. This concept was so new not even the teachers fully understand how to teach the class. I would hear them use terms such as exponential factors, and immediately I tuned out because my memory banks had not developed language that would connect definitions to the pictures they were trying to convey. I then convinced myself that I could not understand this new concept, so listening became deafening. My grades soon reflected I was not hearing what was being taught even though I was present in the room. Fortunately, I was not the only one struggling with this new experiment which was later scrapped. Listening is an auditory function that most can pick up naturally by listening to others communicate.

Revelation 2:7 says, *"He who has an ear to hear, let hear what the Spirit says to the churches."* This implies there are different levels of hearing. Hearing what everyone hears who understands the language, but and the level of hearing that is not on the surface but is hidden takes and must have a spiritual ear or hearing to know the depth of the intent of the message. There are mysteries of the Kingdom of God only understood with the hearing of the Holy Spirit. Some are content to hear at only a theological level that engages the mind, useful only for debate. The level heard by the hearing of the Spirit hears what God wants the mature believers to hear. When hearing with a spiritual ear, one moves from listening only with natural senses we are all comfortable using to a different language that is not taught with natural wisdom. This hearing comes to those who are hungry for better communication than surface speculation.

The hearing I am speaking of comes out of intimacy. The language of intimacy is perhaps more caught than taught. It is similar to couples who spend their lives together, and words are not sufficient or necessary, but they know the thoughts of one another.

Every person hears differently based on their love language or sometimes called God language. One's own God language is based on how they are wired or understand. Romans 10:17 says, *"Faith comes by hearing, and hearing by the word of God"* (NKJV). This is the key verse most will use to understand the development of hearing. All the ways I will mention will be directly connected to the Word of God. There are a number of ways we hear the Word. I will list just a few so you can get an idea of how you may develop your hearing through the Word or identify your God language.

JESUS USED PARABLES

Parables or stories are used to help people hear the central message of what He wanted to convey to the hearers. In Matthew 13, the use of examples was a key to developing hearers. Each type of soil produced a different result in hearing. If the heart or the soil was free from hardness and other intruding seeds, like thistles, then the ground could hear or produce the maximum potential of harvest. Having a tender heart toward the Lord is perhaps the most important trait to have in hearing Him. Notice in verse 22 that *"the cares of the world and the deceitfulness of riches choke the word, and it proves unfruitful"* (ESV). Cares of life comes from a Greek word *merizō* meaning a divided mind.[1] It's not about a busy mind but a mind that has not fully committed to believing and receiving the truth. This is a mind still open for doubt and other voices to convince them in the opposite direction.

OBEDIENCE TO THE WORD

Obedience implies we have heard and are acting upon what we have heard. James 1:23-24 says, *"For if anyone who is a hearer of the word and not a doer, he is like a man observing his face his natural face in a mirror; for he observes himself, goes away, and immediately forgets what kind of man he was"* (NKJV). There is nothing doing what you have just heard to lock it into your life habits.

I always seemed to learn better when I was allowed to have my hands on something after I had listened. My listening turned into hearing after I was able to do what I was listening to. Once we hear the word, if it doesn't have an application fairly soon after our exposure to it, then we tend not to retain and simply move on to the next thing that will occupy our attention.

John 8:32 says, *"You shall you know the truth, and the truth shall make you free"* (NKJV). I find the only truth that makes me free is not the truth I hear but the truth I apply. Information without application causes us always to be learning but never coming to the knowledge of the truth (2 Tim. 3:7). By applying the Word to a particular area of life we are facing, it solidifies the truth so much in us that we not only contain but also retain the life of that Word. It's not just being able to quote a particular passage; that verse becomes life to your spirit, and you will be able to recall it the next time you step out in faith.

THROUGH YOUR THOUGHTS

Psalm 40:5 tells us, *"Your thoughts toward us cannot be recounted to You in order; if I would declare and speak of them, they are more than can be numbered"* (NKJV).

Jeremiah 29:11 says, *"I know the thoughts that I think toward you, says the Lord, thoughts of peace and not of evil, to give you a future and a hope"* (NKJV).

Our thoughts are like packets of potential. In a flash, thoughts can paint a picture that a thousand words would be needed to explain. Thoughts can be shortcuts to hearing because we can have a thought in a nanosecond that perhaps would take hours of teaching to explain. Thoughts don't need words to process. We can develop healthy thoughts by keeping our minds free from toxic conversations and perversions. We can practice having daily thoughts of the Lord by choosing a topic or Bible verse and simply musing over it and give time for the meditation to soak into our consciousness.

EXTERNAL CONFIRMATIONS

In First Kings 18:44, Elijah waits for a sign after his declaration that the drought was ending when he saw a cloud coming out of the sea. Elijah was in an intercessory position until he saw the cloud. David waited for a sign of sound moving in the tops of mulberry trees before he would attack the Philistines (2 Sam. 5:24). Some are able to hear God through various types of signs. Again, the basis of hearing is by the Word. If we are not regularly grounding ourselves in the Word, then we are in danger of being deceived by signs alone.

THROUGH WORSHIP AND ADORATION

In Acts 13:2 we read, *"As they ministered to the Lord and fasted, the Holy Spirit said, 'Now separate to Me Barnabas and Saul for the work to which I have called them"* (NKJV).

It is in times of worship while our hearts are turned toward the Lord when we clearly hear the voice of the Lord. It's not because God is not speaking at other times, but because we are fully leaning into His presence to hear through tender hearts devoted to adoring Him. It should not come as any surprise as to why we normally worship before hearing the preached message. Hosea 10:11 says, *"Judah (meaning praise) shall plow, and Jacob shall break his clods"* (KJV). It is the praise of the Lord that many times gives us the breakthrough or perhaps the breaking the hard clods of the heart so the coming seed will have a place to be planted.

Worship aligns Heaven and earth, so we have a more open Heaven to hear. When we are following the protocol of Heaven, we then can hear what the Spirit is saying to the Church. Hearing allows us to read the Word with the same spirit as those who received the Word originally.

In the original language, the word "hear" stresses a physical action applied to what we heard for the finishing touch of hearing. My wife, Diane, will wait to see if I am moving toward what she asked me to do to determine if I actually heard or only listened. If I am not responding she will ask; "Are you listening?" When we hear without a response, it is more likely we have only listened. If we truly heard the Holy Spirit say something, it should motivate us to respond so we can receive more instruction.

THROUGH PRAYER

Romans 8:26 says, *"Likewise the Spirit also helps in our weaknesses. For we do not know what we should pray for as we ought, but the Spirit Himself makes intercession for us with groanings which cannot be uttered"* (NKJV).

For me, prayer is not a monologue, but more of a dialogue. I expect to hear something in return with my praying. Even when I am not asking for anything, I can still hear personal encouragement and love coming back into my soul. I am encouraged to know prayer is not a private interaction, but instead, the Holy Spirit is praying and cheering me on in the process. He wants me to succeed as much as I do.

When we partner with the Holy Spirit, we will be able to hear from Heaven. There are times when people just vent to God in prayer. They are pouring out their hearts not really expecting to hear a response mainly because they are not listening in those moments as much as they are doing all the talking. I will usually hear myself pray a verse of Scripture that was made alive to me as I was praying. This is how I hear through prayer. The Holy Spirit praying through me in English is my answer I needed to hear.

Jesus reminded the disciples that when the Holy Spirit came, He would take of Jesus/Word and give it to us; so the Holy Spirit will always speak through the Word. Hebrews 1:1-2 says, *"God, who at various times and in various ways spoke in time past to the fathers by the prophets, has in these last days spoken to us by His Son, whom He has appointed heir of all things, through whom also He made the worlds"* (NKJV). Speaking through prayer will be divinely connected to the relationship with Jesus, and if the Holy Spirit is allowed to participate, He will most certainly speak through the Son or the Word of the Son. Jesus said in John 6:63, *"The words that I speak to you are spirit, and they are life"* (NKJV).

Prayer stirs words of life and spirit, and these Words take on a life entity of their own. What you hear in prayer has life attached, and when you hear them in faith, they begin to be implanted in your spirit preparing for the time they will reproduce long after your memory of the moment has faded.

INCREASE OUR FAITH

We have thus far learned that faith comes by hearing and hearing through the word. One cannot increase their ability to hear without increasing their faith. The two work in tandem much like the Word works in tandem with the spirit; I call them the Dynamic Duo The Word without the spirit is a dead letter (2 Cor. 3:6). Faith is like a large muscle: the more it is used, the stronger it becomes. Though the muscle has potential to move heavy weights, the potential is only maximized when it is used. Hebrews 5:14 says, *"Solid food belongs to those who are of full age, that is, those who by reason of use have their senses exercised to discern both good and evil"* (NKJV). Faith is not a noun, but a verb, and it is supposed to see action.

In Luke 17:5-10, the apostles said to the Lord, *"Increase our faith"* (NKJV). Jesus uses two stories to convey the answer to their question. Perhaps they thought Jesus would pray for them or lay His hands on them to impart the desired increase.

The first story is the mustard seed analogy comparing the act of plucking up the mulberry tree and casting it into the sea. The point being the size of faith is not the issue but the strength. Mustard seed is known to be one of the smallest seeds, and yet it produces plants that grow exponentially to its size and weight. The quality of faith is measured by the purity and unwavering strength connected to it. It is the person operating in faith more than faith itself. If the heart moving in faith is without mixture, then the potential of faith can be fully extended.

The second story Jesus uses to explain an increased faith to the apostles comes through servanthood. They understood the culture of servants and the code of conduct for servants. Jesus was saying if the servant comes in from the field, you wouldn't tell him to sit at the table and be served; no you would tell him to wash himself and serve the table. Notice verse 10, *"when you have done all those things which you are commanded, say, 'We are unprofitable servants. We have done what was our duty to do'"* (NKJV). The lesson in this second story is packed into this one thought; when you only do the minimal as expected, there is no increase in faith.

Faith is increased when we are extended beyond just attending a few meetings or having a belief system. Faith is seen as what we do with what we believe or what we do with the revelation we have. One can have a huge memory of Scripture, study theology, and understand mysteries of the kingdom and still not have faith. Studying the Scripture is the minimal act of faith but it doesn't increase faith until the word learned during studying is applied and depended upon.

I personally know people who are brilliant apologists, but they don't have faith beyond the minimal measure that we are all given. Their faith has not been tested to cause it to be strengthened. One reason to desire an increase of faith is to extend influence and demonstrate the kingdom of God. One last thought about increasing your faith: is simply don't run from challenges, but embrace them and let your faith be strengthened in the process. When we take the past of least resistance to our faith; eventually we will have an anemic faith.

GOD IS JUST, BUT IS HE FAIR?

In Matthew 25:14-30, Jesus is giving the parable of the talents. This story has many cause and affects woven in the comparison of three servants. Each servant was given a sum of money called talents. Each one was given different amounts according to their ability. The ability was no doubt based on their past stewardship.

When the master returned, there were rewards for their faithfulness (remember faith comes by hearing the Word) with what had been given to them. The one who had the most received a reward based on investing what was entrusted to him. The one with the three had likewise received his reward. When the master gave the person the one talent, it was because of the servant's past performance. The servant's excuse was that he did not want to lose what was given to him for safekeeping. Fear seemed to motivate him instead of a vision for an increase. He claimed to know the master, but he was deceived thinking that the master viewed the investment as one to be hidden and not invested. Obviously, he did not hear but only listened. Had he heard fully, he would have understood his master intended for him to step out in faith and risk losing it, but ultimately, doing nothing accomplished what he feared.

Take note of verse 29: *"For to everyone who has, more will be given, and he will have abundance; but from him who does not have, even what he has will be taken away"* (NKJV). The point I want us all to see is if we don't engage and employ what we are hearing, it will be taken from us. Based on the last performance of hearing is what we will be entrusted with. For one to develop the ability to hear clearly, they start with not just listening but doing what they hear. If I am faithful in doing what I hear, then more will be given to me to sow at a higher level.

Jesus said in Luke 8:17-18: *"For nothing is secret that will not be revealed, nor anything hidden that will not be known and come to light. Therefore take heed how you hear"* (NKJV).

Hearing actually means we have an encounter. It is experiential not just auditory. We can forget fairly easily what we hear with the natural senses but what was heard in your spirit never leaves you. Although it may not be at the forefront of your mind, it is deposited upon the hard drive of your spirit. The Holy Spirit will bring back to your remembrance when you need it.

Paul says in First Corinthians 14:8, 10, *"For if the trumpet give an uncertain sound, who shall prepare himself to the battle? ...There are, it may be, so many kinds of voices in the world, and none of them is without signification"* (KJV). Paul was actually talking about several different trumpet sounds throughout the year, but particularly the Trumpet to the Feasts. But also there were trumpet calls that could have been a call to arms, signaling for their preparedness. If one could not distinguish the blasts of the trumpet, they would not be ready for the next event to break. The casual listener could not have determined if it was a call to war or simply a call for evening prayer.

The attentiveness to the voice indicates how close and how much we love the voice or sound. Psalm 89:15 declares, *"Blessed are the people who know the joyful sound! They walk, O Lord, in the light of Your countenance"* (NKJV). Blessed or happy are those who know the joyful sound. The word joyful sound is distinct meaning to split the ear or to open the ear. There is a sound, and then there is the joyful sound. This sound brings one to attention.

Those who are casual in giving attention to the Holy Spirit will miss the subtleties of the Spirit. The details are in the relationship we have with someone we pay attention to. Jesus said in John 10:4 that His sheep knew His voice. The key word is the personal identity to His sheep. His voice is known not just listened to. Knowing the voice not only implies voice recognition but understanding the one speaking.

INFORMATION OVERLOAD

We're in a time right now when we can choose to "hear" the "news" 24-7 from all different sources and a variety of people, each with their own biases and agendas. Anyone who draws from these personal experiences and opinions will load up their minds with mixed seed. Confusion soon begins to creep in, and after a while, we just stop hearing and casually practice scanning with a loose filter. Not only are we supposed to take caution how we hear, but we are also told to guard what we hear. What we hear can eventually affect how we hear.

Skepticism is pretty much the filter of our day. When something of truth is sounded out skepticism has the first skim at the truth. We are taught from secular institutions to question everything and not be quick to believe anything. From a secular position, that is probably not a bad thing. However, we cannot allow the skepticism to bleed over into our spirit to the point of not being able to respond to the joyful sound of truth quickly.

The drone of information can be so overwhelming to the point we can't take it anymore. It is easy to fall into what I call Familiarity of Faith Syndrome. This is when we become so familiar hearing the Word preached and taught that we lose the sense of awe of what we are hearing. Those who teach the Word can fall into this sedative of teaching information, feeling like we are doing everything right as if it exempts us from the most important part—to step out in faith and do what we are teaching. I personally know some who are stimulated intellectually by the Word, and yet not challenged to engage in and believe it as a living letter only, but to be lived out daily.

Jesus was giving a high compliment about John the Baptist in Matthew 11:11. Jesus was explaining to those listening how there was not anyone like John who had been born. Then, at the outset, it appears He took away the honor He just gave John when He said, *"He who is least in the kingdom of heaven is greater than he [John]"* (NKJV). Jesus was pointing to the new covenant that had not been completed. John had served in a high place of honor with his message on repentance. Jesus was the bridge between the old and the new. Those who entered the kingdom were greater than the one who preached about it. The new covenant was the entrance to step into the operation of the gifts of the spirit. Jesus makes the point clear that those who enter into the Kingdom and step into faith are greater than those who only preach about.

I remember when the Holy Spirit challenged me concerning my familiarity of faith. It was a Friday evening, and I was invited to speak at the church that was hosting a special meeting on the prophetic gift in the marketplace. I was encouraging people how they could be sensitive to the Holy Spirit at all times even while in the grocery store. I was giving examples how one could see a need and feel compassion welling up inside and then step into faith for the prophetic word or miracle to happen. In the middle of this thought, the Holy Spirit brought conviction to my heart. He reminded me that I hadn't done this in a while. While speaking, I realized I had substituted talking about the Kingdom without entering into the Kingdom by demonstrating the faith of what I was teaching.

After the meeting, Diane and I along with a few people from the meeting went to dinner at a nice restaurant. A young man who appeared to be our server approached us. Before he could enter into his mantra of a server, I said, "What school are you attending?" He sheepishly answered as if to tell me that may not be any of my business. I then said to him, "You want to change majors but are afraid if you do, you will lose the financing for your degree, but the Lord wants me to tell you to pursue the major that is on your heart, and the Lord will provide for it." He was really puzzled by now. He told us at the table that he was in accounting at the moment but really wanted to change majors to political science.

His father, who was an accountant, was absolutely against the idea and told him if he changed majors, he would not pay for it. The young man was blown away and still trying to process what had just happened while he took our order. I immediately felt the pleasure of the Lord invigorating my soul. Stepping past the point of only talking about the Kingdom and into living in that realm, brought me back to the reality that information without demonstration can make one spiritually lazy and too familiar with teaching and deceive oneself into thinking he is doing the stuff.

THE POWER OF PRESSURE

Most of us will rightfully admit to not liking pressure. For the most part, we try to avoid pressure. We say things like, "I don't want to be under any pressure to do that." I offhandedly commented when I was tired after a long week of ministry, to the Lord about how hard the pressure was. I was blindsided by what came next. The Lord reminded me of how many parables in Scripture had to do with pressure.

In Matthew 9, Jesus explains the principle of the wineskins. Everyone during that time was aware of this saying that you can't put new wine into old wineskins because the pressure from the new wine would burst the old skin. The old skin could not handle the fresh expanding wine. The old wineskin had to be renewed to adjust to the new wine. I got the message loud and clear, which was if you are going to be able to handle the new wine—a type of the Holy Spirit—I was going to have to make pressure my friend, and not my enemy. I knew I needed a different perspective of pressure if I was going to cooperate with the Holy Spirit.

Just think for a moment of all the things that work with pressure. Your blood flows through your body due to pressure, and if you don't adjust to the pressure, it is detrimental to your body. The water that flows uphill to your house would not enter the pipes without pressure. Hydraulic fluid systems use pressure to power equipment that can do the work of a hundred men. In Philippians 3:7-14, the apostle Paul understood how to flow with pressure and against it. He describes it by saying he is *"forgetting what lies behind and straining forward to what lies ahead, I press on toward the goal for the prize of the upward call of God in Christ Jesus"* (ESV).

I have since learned that pressure is not my enemy. I use to think that grace was given to help me avoid pressure, but now I see grace helps pressure flow through me. I am no longer under pressure, but pressure is under me helping me accomplish things my flesh would resist. I would not be writing this book at this minute if it were not for the pressure I placed myself under to complete it. Without pressure, I would likely procrastinate finishing it.

A pastor friend of mine asked me a direct question, as to why other churches did not invite him to speak. I tried to wrangle out of the question, but he persisted wanting an answer. He was a brilliant scholar when it came to knowing the doctrines of the Word. I finally was able to tell him, "After you finish your message, you feel good about what you have done, but the truth is you are only halfway finished. After you are finished teaching, you should demonstrate the Word and not just talk about it because First Corinthians 2:1-4 says We are not to come with words of men's wisdom but instead in the demonstration of the spirit. I explained next time when you are finished preaching, prophesy over the people. He suggested it would be a lot of pressure to do that, but he did understand the Word said we should desire to prophesy. His perception of pressure was anything he was not comfortable with or had experience with.

When Peter steps out of the boat after hearing Jesus bid him to come, he stepped out in faith, but immediately started feeling the external pressure of the waves around him. Peter may have felt the pressure to succeed from those still seated in the boat. Peter lost his focus on Jesus, and his mind took over; he became stressful and cried out to Jesus.

When pressure is not focused toward a target, it becomes stress. Stress is when we don't know how to use pressure as an advantage, and it becomes stressful. Stress depletes the soul, but when we flow with pressure, it can be invigorating. Stress is seeing self with all its weakness and then concluding the results are all on you.

I have been overwhelmed at times when after a long evening of preaching I look out to see the long line of hungry hearts waiting to be prayed over and prophesied to. The reason for the stress is because I am thinking about me and not relying on the turbo kick of the Holy Spirit once I start. It is only stress when the focus is upon me and how tired or inadequate I feel, but each time I have to remind myself, my Father in Heaven loves these people more than I could ever possibly love them. I purposely lay down any reputation I think I have and simply become a servant that is bought and paid for by His precious blood of His Son and I don't own myself. Each time I refuse to let my soul become lazy and take the easy path out, I see amazing healings and prophetic revelations I would not have seen had I reflected on me alone. I have found all He needs is a willing heart and for me to take the first step what I call the "Point of no return."

I think Peter probably had that moment of the "point of no return" when he stepped out of the boat. Though it was not a perfect launch, he still moved forward toward Jesus. Stress will talk you out of faith in a moment's notice, but when you are committed to allowing pressure to work through you, then all you need is to take the first step so you won't back down. Commit your heart to run toward the battle, not from the challenge. Running from the opportunity is a guarantee of coming up empty-handed, but moving toward the call to action has a better chance of success, and when you are finished you will have greater confidence for the next conquest.

The anointing will prompt us, and we may not feel anything until there is a need to release the pressure of the Holy Spirit finding a focused target and move in faith. To keep the pressure focused, keep in mind the Holy Spirit wants us to succeed as much as we do. Secondly, keep the motive and the main objective in view and do not let the pressure be about you—if it does, it will result in stress and anxiety. Philippians 4:6-7 tells us, *"Be anxious for nothing, but in everything by prayer and supplication, with thanksgiving, let your requests be made known to God; and the peace of God, which surpasses all understanding, will guard your hearts and minds through Christ Jesus"* (NKJV). Supplications are very specific focused prayers that target the issue. When praying with pressure, the focus is very narrow and focused. Notice that peace follows this kind of prayer as opposed to having anxiety.

Philippians 2:5-6 gives a clue how Jesus functioned with pressure without pressure being over Him. Jesus chose to not make it about himself or his reputation. He made himself of no reputation and took on the form of a servant. This is why Jesus could be among the Pharisees without them having any power over Him because He was not worried about His reputation. Whoever we are trying to impress is the one we have given power over us.

Many years ago, I was approached by a group of influential people in my church to join an organization of ministries. I went to a couple of meetings and soon discovered I was an outsider. I felt like a foreigner who did not know the language much less the culture. Many of them were handing me business cards as fast as I could take them. I felt like I was in a multilevel sales convention. I was told if I did not align with them, I would not have the Lord's favor on my life or my church. I was also told if I didn't join, I would never be able to publish any books, although at that time I had not written any. I was feeling the pressure for sure to join the group. If I had joined, it would have been solely for the purpose of pleasing a few people who wanted to use me as an access to the same group. When I decided not to join, I was punished by all their friends and became an outcast from any social gatherings. I can honestly say that was one of the best decisions I ever made. Making myself of no reputation kept me from the pressure of those who were seeking to make a name for themselves. Today, I head up a network of churches and ministries committed to loving and caring for one another without any motivation except to see each reach their God-given potential.

When people exert pressure, invariably there will be a competitive spirit inside those circles of influence. Along with a competitive spirit, comes a comparative one as well by comparing one another and only valuing skill sets and not the relationship. Social pressure was what Jesus stayed away from, and it allowed Him to flow with the pressure and promptings of the Holy Spirit. Inside every organization, there are sincere people who can avoid the pitfalls of stress caused by a few who have personal agendas. Jesus did not avoid being among them; He only avoided succumbing to their kind of pressure.

BIOSPHERE II

Some years ago, scientists from the University of Arizona located in Oracle Arizona, began experimental science to create a perfect ecological system. The idea was to have a closed and highly monitored environment for creating plant growth. Their thought was to eliminate any resistance to plant life activity. It would be a sort of utopia for living things. Things grew at an enormous pace. One problem arose, however, concerning the fast growth of the trees. In this perfect environment, there was no wind. They discovered the trees had very weak and shallow roots without wind resistance. Without the wind, the trees didn't grow the necessary strength to hold the growth potential. After a while, the trees would just fall over for lack of root depth.[2]

My point here is that testing and pressure can produce positive results. Children who grow up without having to develop problem-solving skills are more likely to feel victimized by every little issue they face in continuing education and tend to drop out of school at a faster rate than those who were challenged by the resistance they encounter.

There is good pressure, and there is bad pressure. The devil will use pressure against us—especially if we are concerned about our reputation. There is nothing wrong with keeping a good reputation, which is a heart of integrity; the problem lies in trying to make a reputation by playing the game just for their approval. Many times the same ones who can approve will be the same ones who will disapprove you, and the reputation you were hoping they would build for you has now been tarnished.

The Bible says *promotion comes from the Lord*. It should always be the Lord who promotes us when we are ready and not done out of manipulation. For instance, it could be the pressure to give someone a prophetic word because they are influential and can help you. You would need to make the distinction between the social stress from people and the pressure of the Holy Spirit. There could be societal pressure for sex, which leads to deceptive perversion and ultimately control by outside forces of your life. Others may feel the pressure by friends to drink alcoholic beverages so you can fit into their circles of influence. If you yield to pressure from what you see in others, you can know it is not the press of the Holy Spirit.

The pressure of the Holy Spirit will restore your soul; the pressure from the religious community will rob your soul. The pressure must lead to seeing fruit in the kingdom of God. If the pressure is to further a ministry or career by yielding to others' expectations, it is the pressure that will consume your energy, and you may feel like you are in burnout mode. Burnout is the failure of not replenishing your spirit from the One who created your spirit. There is great delight and joy which brings strength when we know in our hearts we have aligned ourselves with the pressure of the Holy Spirit and not the stress of others.

THE HEARING TEST

Matthew 7:24-28 is typically called the parable of the wise and foolish man. Jesus begins the contrast of these types of men by saying; *"Whoever hears these sayings of Mine, and does them, I will liken him to a wise man"* (Matt. 7:24 NKJV). In reality, the core of the message is about hearing the Word. He connects hearing to doing what was heard.

Here is the contrast between two men who evidently heard the same instructions but came away with very different outcomes.

The first man was said to be wise because he built a house on a rock foundation and the elements of wind and rain along with a flood hit the house, but the house stood firm. The second man built a similar house, but the only difference was the foundation. The same elements of rain, wind, and a flood came, but the house was demolished. The foundation of the house is key, but Jesus connects this to hearing. Perhaps the one who was wise heard explicit details as to what he should do. The foolish man heard but possibly only heard about building and took upon himself to fill in the rest of the details.

When hearing the Word, whether it is auditory or through reading, look for the details that could make the difference between success and failure. The test of hearing is one of the first lessons we need to learn to survive in a stress-filled world. His voice brings peace, but only when we do exactly what He is saying will it bring success. The more details we pick up on in developing a hearing gift, the better.

I was helping my dad build a cabinet when I was a young teenager. He wanted me to learn how to measure a board and cut it using the power saw. He called out to me, "Cut it 28 and a quarter inches from the inside mark of your pencil." I pulled out the tape measure, and saw 28 and a bunch of little marks after it. So I marked the board and cut it, feeling proud of my accomplishment. When my dad put the board in place, it was too short. He said to me, "Did you cut it exactly what I called out to you?" I answered, "Close to the 28, just a little mark away from it." After a stern talking to about not wasting lumber and a lesson on reading a tape, I realized details matter and how we hear can determine if we get all the details needed to get the job done.

HEARING AND ENCOUNTERING

The first time I was in Mexico in the early 80s, I was asked to minister at a conference. The church was about eight hundred strong at the time, and the place was packed. I was sitting in the front row and noticed several humongous speakers on the platform. The church and the culture were fairly new to me. I remember thinking, "Lord, I'm so thankful to be here and get a front row seat" because I could see the line of people out the door hoping to get a seat anywhere.

When the band hit that first note, I immediately could tell I was in a position to encounter something great. I ceased hearing with my ears and started encountering—my shirt was actually vibrating from the sound coming through the speakers. I ceased hearing and processing mentally what was happening—now, I was having palpitations. The base speaker felt like it was inside of me. The sound was moving toward me as if we were having a meeting right there. I was now experiencing the music and not just processing it with my external ears.

The idea of hearing is not just receiving information, but to have an encounter with what you hear and with the one you hear from. Adam and his wife heard the sound of the Lord walking in The Garden, and they hid because they no longer could hear with intimacy and receive refreshing. Sin had changed their behavior and their desire to meet with God. The word encounter means to have a meeting. The encounter was for the purpose of refreshing them, but instead, they hid from encountering His presence. Shame comes from unresolved sin and causes one to hide from hearing what should have brought relief from shame.

Hearing is actually the idea of encountering or having a meeting. The story of when Jesus came to Mary and Martha's house reflects this.

Mary wanted to be at the feet of Jesus and hang on His every word. Martha wanted to be there as well but did not position herself to hear. She was filled with the cares of life (divided mind) and missed the encounter—although she perhaps could hear Jesus from the kitchen. The difference was Mary heard, but encountered not only the words but also, the One who is speaking. When you encounter what you are hearing, you will not miss details because you are not just hearing the conversation but receiving the heart from where the words originated. An intimate heart will always hear more closely than a closed heart.

When the Lord speaks to us, we cease trying to hear with our physical senses, we are instead encountering His Presence, and that is when transformation comes. The renewing of the mind that Romans 12:2 refers to happens in this kind of meeting, where the Word and the spirit is meeting, and you are encountering.

"His Word became flesh," He lived out His Word on the earth, fleshed it out, walked it out, and lived it out entirely on the earth. By the same token, His Word is so alive inside us, that when we hear or encounter it, it vibrates within us, transforming us. The Bible talks about those who are born again commit their living out His word by being a doer and not a listener only. But when you encounter the revelation of the power of the One living in you and you can hear Him, you can say in the name of Jesus, "Devil, get away from me! The greater One, the Word alive in me, the same Word that cast you out of Heaven is the same Word speaking through me now!" This comes from a faith-filled position, and the position determines your authority.

I was blessed to have a mother who knew the importance of developing the hearer in me while still a teenager. Every morning before I left for school, she insisted I pull out a card from what was called the

Promise Box that was kept on the kitchen table right alongside the salt and pepper and napkins. The Promise Box consisted of small cards with Scriptures on them. Each morning she made sure I had a promise for the day, and I had to read it out loud to everyone. One morning I said, "Mom, I don't think this is really God. I mean it's kind of like I'm reading a fortune cookie." She said, "What is on the card isn't written by somebody in China. This Scripture is written by the Word Himself." *Okay.* So I pulled out a card and recited the verse.

"Now I want you to memorize it," Mom said. We had to read it out loud in front of the family. And then during the day, something would happen, and I would remember the verse. I had the feeling like I had someone on my side to help in any situation. Over the years, the Word became more than something I memorized; the Word has become a living letter in my heart.

TREASURE OF THE HEART

Psalm 119:11 says, *"Your word I have treasured in my heart, that I may not sin against You."* In other words, His word is to be as a rich treasure that we keep in our hearts—so close that it is part of our very being. When we consider something of great value, we want to keep it safe and secure. We place it somewhere it can't be stolen or damaged. How much more is the Word of God—so the safest most secure place is in our hearts? From there, we draw life physical and spiritual life.

Lord, we confess that You are the Word made flesh, and now You live inside all of us. I ask for the readers who read this through faith that they would develop a strong sense of the power in each one of them. Develop us to hear with the same spirit the early apostles heard with and to act according to Your word. Let the words of our mouths and the meditation of our hearts be acceptable in Your sight. Help us to allow the pressure of the Spirit to flow without obstruction. Deliver us from the stress in our lives, and yet embrace the pressure that moves us toward Your targets. Amen!

CHAPTER 10

CALLED TO BE
A PROPHETIC PEOPLE

HEBREWS 9:11-12 TELLS US, *"Christ came as High Priest of the good things to come, with the greater and more perfect tabernacle not made with hands, that is not of this creation, not with the blood of goats and calves but with His own blood He entered the Most Holy Place once and for all, having obtained eternal redemption"* (NKJV).

The power of redemption began the moment Jesus, the Lamb of God, presented His own blood on the mercy seat in Heaven and what had been stolen from people of the covenant began the process of restoration. The double portion is a term many use as an amount to be paid back after a loss. The double portion is more than a measurement; it is a position of authority. Deuteronomy 21:17 says, *"He shall acknowledge the firstborn, the son of the unloved, by giving him a double portion of all that he has, for he is the beginning of his strength; to him belongs the right of the first born."*

The position of the firstborn son in a Jewish family was an important placement of authority. In today's government of the family, he would be called an executor of the estate. An executor is responsible for carrying out all the wishes or of a will left behind after a death. He would make sure all the heirs of the estate are given their rightful portions according to the will. In the same way, Jesus is our Elder Brother and holds the executor position over the family of God. Romans 8:29 says, *"For whom He foreknew, He also predestined to be conformed to the image of His Son, that He might be the firstborn among many brethren"* (NKJV). The firstborn son was also to receive His double portion first, and then the rest of the family would receive theirs.

Hebrews 12:23 says, *"To the general assembly and the church of the firstborn who are registered in heaven, to God the Judge of all, to the spirits of just men made perfect"* (NKJV). We are called the "Church of the Firstborn," and we know Jesus is the head of the church (Col. 1:18); again, that puts Jesus as the executor of all that the Father possesses which is everything. The only begotten of the Father was also present at creation (Col. 1:15) and is now the restorer of the breach that Adam created through disobedience, but through the obedience of God's only Son, restoration of the family is in progress and in process. We must learn how to pursue what was lost to overtake it and recover into our family legacy for the next generation.

Romans 8:17 tells us, *"If children, then heirs—heirs of God and joint heirs with Christ, if indeed we suffer with Him, that we may also be glorified together"* (NKJV). If you are in the Church of the Firstborn; you are an heir to receive what is in His will for you. He is placing a hunger in our hearts to seek first the Kingdom of God to find all that has been willed to us just waiting for us to claim our inheritance and then proclaim the change it has made in our lives.

THE READING OF THE WILL

In Acts 1:4-5 we read, *"Being assembled together with them, He commanded them not to depart from Jerusalem, but wait for the Promise of the Father, 'which' He said 'you have heard from Me; for John baptized with water, but you shall be baptized with the Holy Spirit not many days from now'"* (NKJV). Jesus was giving them a clue as to what the inheritance would be. The Promise of the Father was a term they understood as Jews as being the inheritance of the family. Though 500 people gathered for the releasing of the inheritance, 380 left before they could receive. Their patience had run out, and maybe they were only there out of a curious heart, not a committed heart. Some want only to be observers, but those who encountered Jesus as more than a teacher were all in for the duration.

Like any High Priest, Jesus took blood in the Holy Of Holies, but this time it wasn't the blood of animals, were only a covering for sin, but He took His own sinless blood into the heavenly Tabernacle and placed His blood on the mercy seat and cleansed sin once and for all, for all who call upon His name and repent and turn from the sin. I can't imagine the sound in Heaven when His blood hit the mercy seat; hell groaned, and Heaven rejoiced because the payment was final.

First Corinthians 15:47 declares where the first Adam became a living being, the last Adam became a life-giving spirit. The first Adam was a receiver of life, and the last Adam was the giver of life. The first Adam failed to subdue and take dominion the last Adam/Jesus subdued and conquered death, hell, and the grave. The last Adam is our Redeemer and our Elder Brother who is restoring all things as originally planned by our Father in Heaven.

Acts 2:15-17 describes the day we received restoration of the family authority. Luke described that moment as wind rushing through the room. They knew He would come but did not know how He would come. Today, many miss out on their inheritance because they did not like how it was delivered. When Jesus placed His blood on the mercy seat, the Holy Spirit filled the room and was giving gifts to those who were waiting in anticipation. They did not know what to make of this gift.

Peter standing up begins to give an explanation. He let everyone know that they were not looking at drunk people because it was too early in the day. It must have looked similar to people who had over-filled themselves with wine. Peter quoted Joel 2:28 saying, *"In the last days, says God, that I will pour out of My Spirit on all flesh [Jew and Gentile]; and your sons and daughters shall prophesy, your young men shall see visions, your old men shall dream dreams"* (NKJV).

Just think with me for a moment, and place yourself inside the upper room. You are waiting for the will to be read so to speak; you are not sure what the God of all creation would give to you, but you know it must be hugely important. Then all of a sudden, you are filled with God Himself through the Holy Spirit, and you hear this is fulfilling the promise over your children that you are going to prophesy. The gift of the Holy Spirit will enable you to prophesy. If it were today, perhaps some would have disappointed thinking they were going to get a boat-load of money or some other material gift.

If we can understand the importance of prophecy, we would know Jesus, our Elder Brother, gave us the tools to accomplish anything. Prophecy is much more than getting or giving a prophetic word. Being prophetic is becoming a partner in creation. God has already created everything that will be created. However, we can speak over things that have been created to come to its potential.

We have the opportunity to step into the role Adam had of subduing and taking governance over creation. Ezekiel sees a vision of dry bones and God asks him what he sees and instructs him to prophesy to the wind, and the bones begin to be restored which was a picture of Israel being restored. He could have given us anything, but the legacy of generational prophecy should be passed on to our children in a way that is kept holy and biblically balanced.

Revelation 19:10 tells us, "…*the testimony of Jesus is the spirit of prophecy*" (ESV). Testimony "means to do it again." It is also a legal term for someone to give witness to something. In this case, prophecy testifies of Jesus the One who gave us the gift of the Holy Spirit and the authority to prophesy. One can learn to prophesy over themselves. You can testify of the healing covenant of Jesus through prophesying over sick bodies. With this testimony, just as Jesus healed while on the earth, we are prophesying or witnessing His healing right now.

In the beginning, nothing changed until someone said something. When God said, "let there be" the Holy Spirit moved in concert with God's voice. I am not saying we are God, but I can conclude from Scripture we are partners with Him in seeing things lost that was originally created, come into His divine order. In many cases, nothing happens because no one is calling out Restore, Restore! The Holy Spirit is waiting for us to declare what has already been decreed so He can move with the Word. John 1:3 tells us, *"All things were made through Him, and without Him nothing was made that was made"* (NKJV). This wonderful gift of the Holy Spirit is now prompting us to prophesy the Word, so things that were made can be once again (read *The Power of Blessing*) restored as it was originally intended. Jesus, the last Adam, has given us the gift to prophesy to things out of order whether it is family, friends, or government.

The principle of the firstborn was that the firstborn was to receive his inheritance first, then his siblings would receive their inheritance. For this to be fulfilled, Jesus would need to receive His inheritance before the outpouring on the Day of Pentecost. Psalm 2:7-8 says, *"The Lord said to Me, 'you are My Son, today I have begotten You. Ask of Me, and I will give you the nations for Your inheritance, and the ends of the earth for Your possession'"* (NKJV). Notice the capitalized pronouns referring to God speaking over His Son and saying He will give Him the nations for His inheritance. This excites me to see that Jesus, our Elder Brother, received His inheritance when He offered His blood, and at that moment, Jesus inherited the nations of the world. To make it more personal, Jesus inherited you and me; we became a gift back to Jesus.

Acts 3:25 says, *"You are sons of the prophets, and of the covenant which God made with our fathers, saying to Abraham, 'And in your seed all the families of the earth shall be blessed'"* (NKJV). In the Old Testament, prophets were far and few between. They lived more of a solitary life, whereas, in the New Testament, all who have been redeemed are filled with the spirit of prophecy.

Though we are not all prophets or function in the gift of prophecy, we all have the Spirit of Christ. Anyone who does not have the Spirit of Christ is none of His according to Romans 8:9. Since the spirit of prophecy is the testimony of Jesus (Rev.19:10), all who carry the name of Christ also carries the testimony of Jesus that entails the spirit of prophecy. The term prophecy means not only to foretell but also a proceeding word. Deuteronomy 8:3 confirms by saying, *"...man shall not live by bread alone; but man lives by every word the proceeds from the mouth of the Lord"* (NKJV).

Man began by the word God spoke over the dirt and man was created, but man became a living being when God breathed into him. Living being is also translated as "speaking spirit." We were created predominately spirit, until the Fall of Man, and man took on more of the mind and will dominance. The redemptive rights of all who are redeemed are to pursue your role as sons of the prophets who were given authority to speak the Word of the Lord to bring things to order and original design.

We began life because of God prophesying over us, and He is saying we are to continue to live by every word that comes from His mouth. The bread He speaks of can come from the written word and or the spoken word based on the foundation of what God has already said. What He said is called the Logos or said word, but when we hear it fresh and speak it out the word becomes a saying word or present word for the moment. What a wonderful privilege for us to have inherited this ability to declare on earth what has already been said or decreed in Heaven.

The point I wanted to make here is the Word is close by in our mouths. Romans 10:6,8 says, *"...'Who will ascend into heaven?' (that is, to bring Christ down from above)... But what does it say? 'The word is near you, in your mouth and in your heart (that is, the word of faith, which we preach)"* (NKJV). Since faith comes by hearing and hearing by the Word, we can see the need to restore our ability to hear through the Spirit so we can become only hearers of the Word, but also sayers of the Word. Nothing is restored until we enforce the victory of the cross—through proclaiming what we have claimed. The enemy cannot resist the Word as a legal power-filled enforcement declaration, but it must be prophesied or spoken in declaration as one who would go before the court and petition the court to make the thief give back what He stole. Your redemptive rights are as real as your citizenship and certainly more eternal.

I would that you all prophesy:

In Numbers 11:16-17, we learn that due to the heavy responsibility Moses carried trying to hear every case brought to him from the people who had yet entered the promised inheritance, God told Moses to gather 70 men of the elders of the tribes and bring them to the tabernacle of meeting. When Moses gathered them to the door of the tabernacle, God came down and talked with Moses and took of the Spirit that is upon Moses and placed the same upon the 70 to bear the burden of the people so Moses would not have to bear it alone. In verse 25 we read, *"Then the Lord came down in the cloud, and spoke to him, and took of the Spirit that was* upon him, and placed *the same* upon the seventy elders; and it happened, *when the Spirit rested upon them, that they prophesied, although they never did so again"* (NKJV).

The initial sign of the Holy Spirit coming on those who would govern the people was prophecy. There were two who didn't come to the tent of meeting—maybe they didn't get the memo—and their names were Eldad and Medad. They were not part of the group where Moses was, and they began to prophesy too. A young man ran to tell Moses about the two who were not present but still received prophecy and Joshua, Moses' assistant, wanted to send someone to stop them but instead, Moses said, *"Oh, that all the Lord's people were prophets and that the Lord would put His Spirit upon them!"* (NKJV). I hope you can see the Lord wants all of us to be prophetic and pray with same prophetic insight.

Our prophetic heritage comes from the Lord. The apostle Paul said in First Corinthians 14:1, *"Pursue love and desire spiritual gifts, but especially that you may prophesy."* In verse 5, Paul again said, *"I wish you all spoke with tongues, but even more that you prophesied; for he who prophesies is greater than he who speaks with tongues, unless indeed he interprets, that the church may receive edification"* (NKJV). From the Old Testament to the New Testament, we have now seen we were intended to be a prophetic people. In some places, they forbid anyone to speak with tongues or prophesy. If that is the case with you, just know you can practice your redemptive rights at home or find a place that values what Jesus has restored to you.

Now to Him who is able to do exceedingly abundantly above all that we ask or think, according to the power that works in us (Eph. 3:20 NKJV).

I hope we can recognize all that has been invested and placed inside of every believer. Just as the Ark of the Covenant in the Old Testament contained the glory of God, so we too contain His glory. God instructed Moses (Hebrews 9:4) to place three particular items inside the Ark that were extensions of His Presence: Aaron's rod that bore fruit; the tablets of the Ten Commandments; and a pot of manna. Aaron's rod represented the authority of his position with God as the High Priest. The Ten Commandments represented the Word of God, and the manna represented how God always wanted to reveal Himself to the people. Inside every believer, as a New Testament Ark of God's Presence, are the same elements of authority, a manifestation of His Word, and the revelation of His glory through the leadership of the Holy Spirit.

You are truly a prophetic person with everything you need to prophesy to any mountain that restricts the will of God in your life and command it to be removed. You have the authority to tell the mountain how big God is instead of telling everyone else how big the mountain is. Prophetic people see opportunities in the problems; pessimist people see everything as a reason to fail.

Lord Jesus, thank You for being our Elder Brother and Redeemer who gives good gifts to the family of God. Help us always to be aware of the activity and the willingness of the Holy Spirit to work through us. Help us never to fall short of the glory You intended for us to have. May we live up to our creative position of being a speaking spirit that will say what You have already said. Give us a fresh image of what it looks like to allow the prompting of the Holy Spirit to flow like water through us. Today, we commit our faith toward being sons and daughters who prophesy. Amen!

CHAPTER II

CALLED—ASSIGNED— EMPOWERED

I WAS EIGHTEEN YEARS OLD the summer before I would graduate from high school. I was working at a fence company during the summer when youth camp came around. I felt strongly that I was to go, but my boss would not let me off since it was the busiest time of the year for his business. I was surprised at my boldness when I told him I had to go to the camp. He replied "I can't guarantee you a job when you get back" and I agreed with him just knowing something was going to happen.

The week moved along, and each service seemed to touch everyone but me. My friends were all being prophesied to, and I seemed to be invisible. The last night of the camp came, and I was sitting on the back row wearing a pink shirt (pink was in at the time) preoccupied with the young lady in front of me when the Holy Spirit stirred me to get serious about my future. I bowed my head and repented for wasting time and being easily distracted. I prayed this prayer; "God, tonight I am willing to become anything You want me to be, I just don't know what that is, please show me tonight."

No sooner had I raised my head when the speaker, Grace Solis, pointed her long bony finger at me and said, "Young man in the back with the pink shirt," I immediately felt the fear of God come over me and probably I was a little afraid of her too. She went on to prophesy, "You have been wanting your own way, but tonight the Lord is calling you to preach the Word without fear or favor of man, you will to nations I will send you and speak under the authority of the Holy Spirit. You will be a troubleshooter to other churches, though the Lord has given you an unusual ability to make money you will lay it down and serve the Lord." I didn't know what to make of all that was said, but the seed was definitely sown and sown deep it was.

I asked my friend sitting next to me what a troubleshooter was. He shrugged his shoulders and said, "I think it is someone who gets shot for causing trouble." I frowned at him and thought that didn't sound good. Maybe it was a warning to behave, all I knew something happened that would affect my life for years to come, though I didn't have the understanding to process all that was spoken over me.

There were four of us young men who were recognized by our pastor as called to preach. His first words to me were, "Don't think that you will preach from my pulpit." Looking back, I see how he was challenging me to stretch my faith. But because the word that was prophesied was deep inside and her voice still ringing in my ears, I set out to test the calling. My pastor challenged me to find my own platform for preaching.

Without any instruction, all I knew to do was to get my Bible and go to the park. I went to Elwood Park in Amarillo, Texas. It was known for not-so-savory people hanging out there. I located a concrete picnic table in the center of the park. All I knew to do was what I had seen on a few televangelist's do. I stood on the table and started to share a simple Gospel message of the love of God. I saw one homeless-looking man approach me thinking the message had interested him; I smiled at him, and he railed at me in a strange guttural voice to leave his park.

Here is where the test of the call started. My first sense was to run not knowing what he would do next, and my confidence level at that point was close to the bottom of the scale. Suddenly, my voice got strong, and I said something to the effect of, "this is Holy Ground, and I have been sent to take it back, and I bind you in the name of Jesus." To my shock, he took off running shouting obscenities at me on the way.

That day I learned there is real and tangible power in the name of Jesus. Though I had gone to church all my life, I wasn't sure if I really had any faith until it was tested. I believe it was possible but not sure I wanted to test the theory. That day it moved from being a theory to reality. Since that time, I have witnessed firsthand the manifested presence of God transform lives beyond what my mind thought could take place. What happened in the park got back to my pastor, and later I was allowed to teach in the church. He wanted to see if I took the calling seriously or was it a passing thing that would fade away, and perhaps it would have faded if I had not taken steps of faith to release what little I had at the time.

CALLED

In Matthew 22, Jesus is sharing a parable of a king who arranged a marriage for his son. The king sent out invitations for guests to come and celebrate the marriage of his son, but they were not willing to come. Again, the king sent out servants to bid them to come to this elaborate feast. One by one, they all made excuses saying they were too busy with their own business to come and they treated the servants of the king harshly. The king was furious at the rejection of his son's celebration. The king sent out his servants a third time to invite anyone they randomly came in contact with.

The wedding hall was soon filled with guests; though they were not the original invited guests, nonetheless, the wedding celebration was ready. When the king came into the hall to see the guests, he saw a man who did not have a wedding garment. When asked where his wedding garment was, the man was utterly speechless. The king ordered the man bound hand and foot and cast out of the wedding hall.

For most of us, we would think it was rude of the king to kick this man out seeing he was invited unexpectedly. But in Jewish tradition, a wealthy person—such as a king—would have a gatekeeper who would pass out garments to everyone who enters. The garment is an outer covering, and it would bear the crest of the king which would speak of all his domain and wealth.[1] For this man to come in without a wedding garment (Matthew 22:11-14) would be an insult to the king. He would, in essence, be saying, "I want your food and to enjoy all the benefits that come from a king, but I don't want your identity instead I want to keep my own identity."

In verse 14, Jesus said, *"Many are called, but few are chosen"* (NKJV). The best translation says many are called, but few will choose. The parable message was about the choice of the king who originally called a specific people who most scholars agree are the Jews. They would not accept His son Jesus as Messiah, and so He sent out invitations to the Gentiles or non-Jews. The second message in the parable was that all were called even the Gentiles.

A calling is an opportunity; it's not a mandate. Someone can boast of being called of God, but my next question to them would be; what are you doing to accept the invitation? All calls have an RSVP attached waiting for a response. A call without a response is a lost opportunity.

I wonder how many have had lost opportunities simply because there was no response or faith attached to the reply. Allow me to give you an example of what I am saying.

I sent a text to a friend inviting him to go to a meeting with me and the space in the car was limited so let me know if you are interested. I didn't hear from my friend, so I asked someone else to go. When it was time to leave my house, my friend who I had originally sent the text to shows up ready to go. It was somewhat awkward, but he realized he needed to respond. In his mind, he had the invitation and was going, but there was no further action on his part to reserve his spot.

Sometimes we sense the call of God in a particular area of service, and yet we never acknowledge we are interested and willing to do what is necessary to move to the next step. For me, going to the park was rather simple and small, but it was my waving my hands saying, "Hey, choose me." I come in contact with people in various cities with similar stories of how they knew God was calling them and they were waiting for someone to put them into their ministry or gifting. The problem with that mindset is we depend on someone else to hear for us, and initially, that is fine, but the next step must be us, or we become codependent the rest of our lives for affirmation or acceptance. You must settle it in your heart and go for it.

IF THIS IS YOU, INVITE ME TO COME

In Matthew 14:28-29, Jesus comes to the disciples walking on water, when Peter sees Him, he says to Jesus, "*'Lord, if it is You, bid me to come to you on the water.' Jesus replied, 'Come'*" (NKJV). Notice Jesus did not say "Peter, you come." He said "come" as a general call to anyone in the boat who would come. Everyone was called, but only Peter chose. It wasn't enough just to have a desire to come; there had to be an act of faith to connect with the desire—or else we can live our whole life with desire without moving into faith.

Faith is not what you believe in; faith is what we do with what we believe in. The invitation is for everyone who has an ear to hear His voice. Once you hear, you cannot un-hear. Activation of any call of God starts with some sort of act of faith or an acknowledgement you got the text/message, and you are accepting the call.

In First Kings 19:19, God tells Elijah to anoint Elisha to take his place. When Elijah approaches Elisha, he is plowing with twelve yokes of oxen, and Elijah passed by and threw his mantle on Elisha. Elisha must have understood what this gesture meant because he said to Elijah in verse 20, *"Please let me kiss my father and my mother, and then I will follow you"* (NKJV). On the surface, it would seem to be an innocuous request, but in that time period, it was understood to mean, after my parents have died and there is no more responsibility for me here at home I will follow you. The response to Elisha's request was very direct; *"Go back again, for what have I done to you?"* (NKJV).

Elijah was telling him don't you understand what just happened to you; in essence, you were just called to follow me, but you want it to be on your terms and your timing and if that is the case, then go back to what you have always been doing. Again, many are called, but not everyone will choose. In this circumstance, Elisha recognized it was going to be now or never and sacrificed a set of oxen representing his determination to burn his bridge of return and served Elijah.

NEXT STEP IS THE ASSIGNMENT

Once I had accepted the call of God, the next step was to learn to serve others. I was given small roles in serving from helping to do manual labor to doing hospital visitations. I received a phone call from my pastor to go visit a young man. So after I got off work, I made my way to a tough neighborhood. Pastor knew nothing of the family only that someone had asked for prayer, so my assignment was to go pray, easy enough and off I went thinking I would be finished in 30 minutes max.

I would soon learn that this assignment would serve to lead me into greater depth of discipline and trust of the Holy Spirit. I knocked on the door and an elderly lady answered, and I told her I was there to see what I assumed was her grandson; she interrupted by asking "are you from AA?" I wasn't quite sure what she was referring to, but I said, "No, I am from the church down the road and was sent here to pray." She scoffed and said, "Prayer ain't gonna help any." I knew I was on shaky ground and I might want to cut this to five minutes. She went ahead and allowed me to come in and showed me where he was. She told me he had slit both of his wrists and heard a voice tell him to feed his blood to the fish and she pointed to a large freestanding fish aquarium in the living room. She motioned for me to proceed to a small, dark bedroom in the back. I wanted to abandon my assignment for something more in line with friendly home visitation.

When I walked into the dingy little room, he was sitting on a twin bed against the wall, and I sat down adjacent to him on another twin bed. His head was lowered, so I started the conversation with, "Hey, how are things going?" to try to break the ice somewhat. Wow! That was not the thing to say, evidently, because he raised his head—which after

I looked at him, I wished he had kept it down. He growled at me like a rabid dog and said, "You don't have any power," and when He said that, I knew it was game on. I said back "I come in the name of the Lord Jesus, and He has all the power in heaven and earth."

I was rather happy with my response, thinking that should do it. Not having any experience in dealing with demonic stuff, I was totally unprepared for what happened over the next two hours. He lunged at me, and I found myself in the middle of the floor with this maniac on top of me threatening to do all sort of things to me. The Holy Spirit reminded of the Word of the Lord to speak back to him, and he would become weak and quiet for a few minutes. I felt the need to test and see if he was free or the demons were just hiding out. I would begin to praise and thank the Lord for His mighty power and love over the two of us. Each time it enraged the demons until we came to the root spirit and when it left, he looked like he was dead. When I started praising again, he seemed to be at peace.

In my assignment, I learned on-the-job-training about the power of the blood of Jesus and trusting the Holy Spirit telling me what to say. After finally dealing with the last demon, suicide, I felt exhausted and walked out of the house thinking of what had just happened. If I had made an excuse to get out of the assignment, I would have missed the encounter with Jesus that evening. I learned that day that inside each assignment there awaits an opportunity. Since that time, I have had numerous confrontations with the enemy, but I gained confidence through the tough moments of serving. Some people spend their lives trying to avoid difficult assignments that are for the purpose of setting them up for their big destiny

Jesus accepted His call when He was baptized by John in Matthew 3:17. There was a voice from heaven saying, *"This is My beloved son in whom I am well-pleased."* His Father was showing His call was beginning to be manifested. Immediately after the baptism, the Holy Spirit leads Jesus into the wilderness to be confronted by the devil. Not only is the call now evident, but the first assignment to resist temptation using the Word.

Take note that Jesus was not released to do any miracles until He had first overcome the testing in the wilderness at which time after overcoming the temptation, He was led again out of the wilderness in the power of the Spirit (Luke 4:14). Jesus began with His assignment to overcome the enemy and to serve. Philippians 2:7 records Jesus as choosing to take on the identity as a bondservant. Matthew 20:28 says, *"The Son of Man did not come to be served, but to serve, and to give His life a ransom for many"* (NIV).

DRESS REHEARSAL

In First Samuel 16, Samuel is sent to anoint the next king to replace Saul after he had disobeyed God and the presence of God had left him. Samuel went through all the sons of Jesse starting with the oldest who was a tall, strapping man who looked very kingly. God tells Samuel not to look at the outward man, but upon the heart, God sees the next king (v. 7). After all the sons had passed by, Samuel is still convinced it was Jesse's house where the next king would come from. Jesse explains there is one more son on assignment in the field taking care of sheep.

Samuel ordered them to bring him. When David arrived, the Lord told Samuel to anoint him. Samuel poured anointing from the ram's horn, and the Spirit of the Lord came upon David from that day forward.

This was David's call, but notice because of the call, the assignments followed the call of God. Verse 14 describes Saul as having a distressing spirit due to the Spirit of the Lord departing from him. David is summoned to play on his harp, and the distressing spirit would leave him. David is then made to be Saul's armor bearer along with playing over at tormented times. David would come back at times to serve his father in tending the sheep especially since his older brothers were in Saul's army.

The interesting thing about assignments is they tend to be more than what they appear to be. Some assignments are for testing obedience and others to teach patience. David's next assignment is more demanding than the first. David learned many things tending sheep before there was a call, and now those skills are being brought out more publicly. One day his father sent him to take some food to his brothers and to bring back news of them (chapter 17:17). On this assignment, David was given an opportunity that would change his life forever.

When David came to the camp to see his brothers, he hears the trash-talking threats coming from the Philistine champion, Goliath. For forty days, Goliath had struck terror in the hearts of the Israeli army. No one accepted his challenge.

David hears the threats differently because he has been called anointed and now this was the ultimate assignment. After David made his way past his brother's accusations for him being there and convincing Saul that he was the guy, David enters the battlefield. He sees the giant through the lens of his preparation for this moment, remembering the encounter with a lion and a bear and his success rate was one hundred percent kill ratio (v. 37). David is not moved by the threats but prophesies the fate of this uncircumcised pagan. David declares his authority comes from the Lord of Hosts (v. 45).

That day Israel scored a huge victory, and David never again went back to his father's house. You would think David would be home free and was coming into his full ministry, but from there, he continued ministering to Saul and later fled from Saul's jealous rage. David had other assignments that taught him skills of leading other men. David led a band of six hundred men who grew in battle strategy until finally he was made a king.

Zechariah 4:10 teaches us not to despise small beginnings. The assignments you serve in may not appear to have anything to do with what you are anointed to do, but by being faithful and obedient, the time will come when you will have your opportunity to soar. Some people never get the opportunity to step into their fullness because they didn't learn to serve in their assignments or didn't like the assignments chosen for them. I didn't always like the math assignments the teacher would send home with me to do. I wish they would give me equations I knew how to do, but the ones I didn't understand took longer to figure out.

Our assignments usually are to stretch our faith or to deal with pride issues. Most of the staff serving with me in my church today started serving in areas of maintenance and other hidden duties. Those who cheerfully served in their assignments, no matter how menial the job, are still with me 20 plus years later. You may be in an assignment right now and not recognize it as an assignment, but whatever you do, serve with a cheerful heart and honor the Lord with the work of your hands and you will prosper.

EMPOWERED

After the call and all the assignments, there comes the time of empowerment. Empowerment is somewhat different from anointing, although there is power with the anointing of the Lord. I see empowerment as two parts: one is the power to do something beyond your natural ability such as with anointing; and secondly, is an authority that releases to act in the power you have received. A good example of this is a car engine has the power to do excessive things, and the transmission is the authority that puts the power in gear to move. In power without authority, you could rev the engine, but it doesn't go anywhere until it is released through authority.

Galatians 4:1-2 says, *"I say that the heir [Jesus] as long as he is a child, does not differ at all from a slave, though he is master of all, but is under guardians and stewards until the appointed time by the father"* (NKJV). This passage refers to Jesus growing up like a normal son and learning under teachers and oversight until the father says it's time to be released into the family business. My point is you might have a huge call on your life, but you are still to submit to the lessons and assignments, so one day you will be released by the Father. If you are without a spiritual father or mother, ask the Holy Spirit to set you into a place where you can grow under good leadership. There are those who try to take the shortcuts because they don't trust oversight to release them in due time and so they waste years wandering as a spiritual orphan.

In John 5:6, Jesus walks into a place called the Pool of Bethesda. It was a pool of water surrounded by five porches. Each porch was full of infirmed people waiting for a miracle. Perhaps each porch gathered people of like malady. They say misery loves company and maybe they spent years sharing their stories of the injustices and disappointments waiting for the angel to come down and stir the water. Tradition says the first one in after the appearance of the angel would be healed.

Jesus approached a man who had been infirmed for 38 years. He asked him if he wanted to be well; the man began to give the excuse he had probably given a hundred times before, reciting that while he is trying to get into the water at the precise time of the water being stirred, someone gets in front of him and he is denied the opportunity for a miracle. Jesus wasn't asking him why he was not healed but asking if the man wanted to be healed. This man was expecting someone to put him into the water. I want to end with this thought. Please don't try to manipulate anyone to do shortcuts before you are ready. Trust the One who called you and who will also qualify you and make you complete in every good work (Heb. 13:21).

Lord Jesus, I ask that You would make us aware You are at work inside us to bring us to fullness. Help us to be delighted in every assignment and not to skip the extra homework. You have redeemed us to pursue, overtake, and recover all that the enemy has stolen from us. Let this book be a reference tool to go after lost children, lost wages, and lost friendships. You are the restorer of the breach and nothing is ever lost only hidden when we partner with You. Thank You for the power of redemption, and help us to empower others to recover as well. Amen!

ENDNOTES

CHAPTER 1

1. "G5117—topos—Strong's Greek Lexicon (KJV)." Blue Letter Bible. Accessed 11 Dec, 2017. https://www.blueletterBible.org//lang/lexicon/lexicon.cfm?Strongs=G5117&t=KJV

2. "H2388—chazaq—Strong's Hebrew Lexicon (KJV)." Blue Letter Bible. Accessed 1 Jan, 2018. https://www.blueletterbible.org//lang/lexicon/lexicon.cfm?Strongs=H2388&t=KJV

3. "H7592—sha'al—Strong's Hebrew Lexicon (KJV)." Blue Letter Bible. Accessed 1 Jan, 2018. https://www.blueletterbible.org//lang/lexicon/lexicon.cfm?Strongs=H7592&t=KJV

CHAPTER 2

1. "G5287—hypostasis—Strong's Greek Lexicon (KJV)." Blue Letter Bible. Accessed 1 Jan, 2018. https://www.blueletterbible.org//lang/lexicon/lexicon.cfm?Strongs=G5287&t=KJV

2. Chuppah source

3. "G5461—phōtizō—Strong's Greek Lexicon (KJV)." Blue Letter Bible. Accessed 1 Jan, 2018. https://www.blueletterbible.org//lang/lexicon/lexicon.cfm?Strongs=G5461&t=KJV

4. "G3540—noēma—Strong's Greek Lexicon (KJV)." Blue Letter Bible. Accessed 4 Jan, 2018. https://www.blueletterbible.org//lang/lexicon/lexicon.cfm?Strongs=G3540&t=KJV

5. "G1984—episkopē—Strong's Greek Lexicon (KJV)." Blue Letter Bible. Accessed 4 Jan, 2018. https://www.blueletterbible.org//lang/lexicon/lexicon.cfm?Strongs=G1984&t=KJV

CHAPTER 3

1. "H5647—`abad—Strong's Hebrew Lexicon (NLT)." Blue Letter Bible. Accessed 4 Jan, 2018. https://www.blueletterbible.org//lang/lexicon/lexicon.cfm?Strongs=H5647&t=NLT

2. "G3623—oikonomos—Strong's Greek Lexicon (NKJV)." Blue Letter Bible. Accessed 4 Jan, 2018. https://www.blueletterbible.org//lang/lexicon/lexicon.cfm?Strongs=G3623&t=NKJV

CHAPTER 4

1. "G1366—distomos—Strong's Greek Lexicon (KJV)." Blue Letter Bible. Accessed 4 Jan, 2018. https://www.blueletterbible.org//lang/lexicon/lexicon.cfm?Strongs=G1366&t=KJV

2. "H8416—tĕhillah—Strong's Hebrew Lexicon (KJV)." Blue Letter Bible. Accessed 4 Jan, 2018. https://www.blueletterbible.org//lang/lexicon/lexicon.cfm?Strongs=H8416&t=KJV

CHAPTER 5

1. "G2222—zōē—Strong's Greek Lexicon (KJV)." Blue Letter Bible. Accessed 4 Jan, 2018. https://www.blueletterbible.org//lang/lexicon/lexicon.cfm?Strongs=G2222&t=KJV

2. "G4053—perissos—Strong's Greek Lexicon (KJV)." Blue Letter Bible. Accessed 4 Jan, 2018. https://www.blueletterbible.org//lang/lexicon/lexicon.cfm?Strongs=G4053&t=KJV

3. "G971—biazō—Strong's Greek Lexicon (NASB)." Blue Letter Bible. Accessed 4 Jan, 2018. https://www.blueletterbible.org//lang/lexicon/lexicon.cfm?Strongs=G971&t=NASB

4. Eye of a needle reference

5. "The Desert Tabernacle." http://www.thedeserttabernacle.com/2011/02/numbers-47-table-of-faces-and-bread-of.html

6. Research on mouse DNA

CHAPTER 6

1. "H7779—shuwph—Strong's Hebrew Lexicon (NKJV)." Blue Letter Bible. Accessed 4 Jan, 2018. https://www.blueletterbible.org//lang/lexicon/lexicon.cfm?Strongs=H7779&t=NKJV

2. "G3441—monos—Strong's Greek Lexicon (NASB)." Blue Letter Bible. Accessed 4 Jan, 2018. https://www.blueletterbible.org//lang/lexicon/lexicon.cfm?Strongs=G3441&t=NASB

3. "G3307—merizō—Strong's Greek Lexicon (NKJV)." Blue Letter Bible. Accessed 4 Jan, 2018. https://www.blueletterbible.org//lang/lexicon/lexicon.cfm?Strongs=G3307&t=NKJV

CHAPTER 7

1. "G692—argos—Strong's Greek Lexicon (NKJV)." Blue Letter Bible. Accessed 4 Jan, 2018. https://www.blueletterbible.org//lang/lexicon/lexicon.cfm?Strongs=G692&t=NKJV

2. Reference for meaning of bosom in biblical times

3. "G4856—symphōneō—Strong's Greek Lexicon (NIV)." Blue Letter Bible. Accessed 4 Jan, 2018. https://www.blueletterbible.org//lang/lexicon/lexicon.cfm?Strongs=G4856&t=NIV

4. "G4012—peri—Strong's Greek Lexicon (KJV)." Blue Letter Bible. Accessed 4 Jan, 2018. https://www.blueletterbible.org//lang/lexicon/lexicon.cfm?Strongs=G4012&t=KJV

5. "G2540—kairos—Strong's Greek Lexicon (NKJV)." Blue Letter Bible. Accessed 4 Jan, 2018. https://www.blueletterbible.org//lang/lexicon/lexicon.cfm?Strongs=G2540&t=NKJV

6. "G5550—chronos—Strong's Greek Lexicon (NKJV)." Blue Letter Bible. Accessed 4 Jan, 2018. https://www.blueletterbible.org//lang/lexicon/lexicon.cfm?Strongs=G5550&t=NKJV

7. "H7725—shuwb—Strong's Hebrew Lexicon (NKJV)." Blue Letter Bible. Accessed 4 Jan, 2018. https://www.blueletterbible.org//lang/lexicon/lexicon.cfm?Strongs=H7725&t=NKJV

8. Reference for use of vessels in biblical times

9. Reference for how wineskins were cared for in biblical times

CHAPTER 8

1. "G225—alētheia—Strong's Greek Lexicon (NLT)." Blue Letter Bible. Accessed 4 Jan, 2018. https://www.blueletterbible.org//lang/lexicon/lexicon.cfm?Strongs=G225&t=NLT

2. "G5611—hōraios—Strong's Greek Lexicon (NKJV)." Blue Letter Bible. Accessed 4 Jan, 2018. https://www.blueletterbible.org//lang/lexicon/lexicon.cfm?Strongs=G5611&t=NKJV

CHAPTER 9

1. "G3307—merizō—Strong's Greek Lexicon (NKJV)." Blue Letter Bible. Accessed 4 Jan, 2018. https://www.blueletterbible.org//lang/lexicon/lexicon.cfm?Strongs=G3307&t=NKJV

2. Reference info for biosphere

CHAPTER II

1. Reference info about Jewish wedding traditions

ABOUT THE AUTHOR

KERRY KIRKWOOD is the founding pastor of Trinity Fellowship in Tyler, Texas. Kerry is known for a strong prophetic ministry. In conjunction with being the founding senior pastor of Trinity Fellowship Church in Tyler, Texas, he is also the director of Antioch Oasis Network of churches and ministries. He has appeared numerous times on Sid Roth's *It's Supernatural* television program, has authored four books, and is a conference speaker at various venues. Kerry is called by many as a "pastor to pastors." He and his wife, Diane, have four children and six grandchildren.